Candy Christmas's

CHRISTMAS

Collection

Recipes, Stories, and Inspiration from Candy's House to Yours

HOWARD
PUBLISHING CO.

Our purpose at Howard Publishing is to:
- *Increase faith* in the hearts of growing Christians
- *Inspire holiness* in the lives of believers
- *Instill hope* in the hearts of struggling people everywhere

Because He's coming again!

Published by Howard Publishing Co., Inc.
3117 North 7th Street, West Monroe, Louisiana 71291-2227

02 03 04 05 06 07 08 09 10 11   10 9 8 7 6 5 4 3 2 1

Edited by Tammy L. Bricket and Dawn M. Brandon
Interior design by LinDee Loveland and Stephanie Denney
Food Photography by Mike Rutherford Studio
Food Stylist, Teresa Blackburn
Portraits by Alden A. Lockridge

Special thanks to Malissa Sanders for her tireless efforts in gathering and typing the
contents of this book.

Library of Congress Cataloging-in-Publication Data

Christmas, Candy, 1961–
    Candy Christmas's Christmas collection : recipes, stories, and inspiration from
Candy's house to yours.
        p. cm.
    ISBN: 1-58229-255-8
    1. Christmas cookery. I. Title.

TX739.2.C45 C35 2002
641.5'68—dc21
                                                        2002024064

Scripture quotations are taken from *The Holy Bible,* Authorized King James Version,
© 1961 by The National Publishing Co.

 FOR BEATRICE HEMPHILL,
MY BELOVED GRANDMOTHER.

Her unwavering faith in Christ has made her a pillar of strength for our family. She is a shining example of the virtuous woman of Proverbs 31. She opens her mouth with wisdom and kindness, fearing the Lord.

Grateful for her example and love, I take this opportunity to rise up and call her blessed. In my quest to be more like Christ, I've discovered that the closer to Him I become, the more of my grandmother I see in myself.

She has a unique way of making each of her children and grandchildren believe they're her favorite (but secretly, I know I really am).

THE CHRISTMAS NAME

I'm often asked about my name, Candy Christmas. Yes, this really is my name. When I was born, my parents named me Carmel Lynn Hemphill. But as my dad peered at me through the window of the hospital nursery, he said, "That's my Candy girl." From that moment, I was called Candy.

Do you believe God has a sense of humor? I do, because in 1987 Candy Hemphill married a young minister named Kent Christmas—and I became Candy Christmas!

The Christmas name came to us from our ancestors, who were German immigrants. They followed their dreams for a better life to America, but at that time, there was friction between our two countries. They thought it would be best to downplay their nationality by changing their name. Having landed in the States on Christmas Day, they took on the name "Christmas" to commemorate the momentous occasion. Consequently, our German name has been lost over the years.

Nearly two centuries later, we're still proudly carrying the Christmas name and legacy, enjoying the bounty of this great nation and the abundant life we have in Christ Jesus.

"I am come that they might have life, and that they might have it more abundantly."

John 10:10

CONTENTS

CONTENTS

CONTENTS

Welcome, friend! I'm so pleased to have you as my guest. Please join me for an intimate journey through my home to an enchanted yuletide in the Christmas family fashion.

Christmas is a special time of year when family and tradition blend together into magical holiday grandeur. It's a time to express love for one another and celebrate the heritage of our faith at the many parties and festive gatherings with those who are dear.

Nestled in the pages of this book, you'll find many of my favorite recipes that have been tried and proven throughout the years. Most of these wonderful delicacies were handed down to me by family members and are as much a part of our holiday tradition as carving Turkey Tom on Christmas Eve.

You'll also find fun candy and craft ideas designed with tiny hands in mind. My children and I love preparing them together, and in doing so, we've made many happy memories, enriched our relationships, and brought special cheer to our holiday.

I'll be sharing with you many entertaining ideas and family holiday traditions, as well as some of my most treasured Christmas memories and miracles. It is my hope that throughout the lines of every page—each story, poem, lyric, or tradition—a common thread will be revealed: The Christmas season is wonderful because we celebrate the birth of the "Wonderful, Counselor, The mighty God, The everlasting Father, The Prince of Peace" (Isaiah 9:6). Without Him the holiday season has no joy. I share with you the experiences of my life only through the light of faith in Christ, because He *is* my life.

So after your majestic pine has been filled with sparkling lights, your home is cheerfully adorned, and your guests are seated for your elegant feast, I hope you'll pause for a moment to say, "Happy Birthday, Jesus. Thank You for all You've done for us."

"For in him we live, and move, and have our being." Acts 17:28

Trimming

TRIMMING
THE TREE

"'Tis the season..." It all begins when the fresh smell of newly cut pine fills the house. Boxes stuffed with ornaments chronicling Christmases past are stacked beside the couch waiting to be emptied and sent back to the attic. White twinkle lights are draped across furniture to keep them from tangling while they're plugged in to be sure every bulb will light when they're strung. Children dance around the room, eagerly anticipating the big event that signals the start of the best season of all. It's Christmastime! And when the tree goes up, the party begins.

the Tree

LIGHTING UP CHRISTMAS

Trimming the tree usually marks the start of the holiday activities in our home. It kindles the first discernible flicker of the Christmas spirit in my children's eyes—a glow that grows brighter as we chatter, laugh, and reminisce about Christmases past. This is a time when the whole family can have fun working on a project together.

We usually have several Christmas trees throughout our home: one in each of the family rooms and in the children's bedrooms. I like to try new decorating ideas on our "fancy" tree in the great room. It stands with its white lights illuminated in front of the picture window for all who pass by to enjoy. We have a more traditional tree in our den especially for my husband and our children, who enjoy a tree with colored lights (like the large bulbs used when I was a child) and old-fashioned ornaments. We like to fill this tree with candy canes of all flavors that we enjoy throughout the season.

My son Nicholas, nine, loves to be involved in every aspect of tree trimming. From assembling our artificial trees to stringing lights and hanging ornaments, he is completely captivated by the whole process. Of course, he has his own idea of just how it should be done. When each tree is "finished," you can tell at a glance where Nicholas has been working. Most of his ornaments hang within a two-foot radius—within his reach from right to left, and from his eye level on down. He takes great pride in his tree-trimming skills, and I would never dampen his spirits; so I praise him as though he's done a professional job. As soon as he leaves the room, I redistribute the decorations more evenly around the tree. So far he has been none the wiser. I wouldn't trade this time with him for anything. I know he won't always be this age, and one day his attention will be drawn to other places and things.

Jasmine, fourteen, is different. She has come to realize that tree trimming isn't all it's cracked up to be. The bottom line is, trimming the tree is a lot of work! She's content to leave untangling wires, checking fuses, changing bulbs, and stringing lights round and round the tree to Nicholas and me.

But when it's time to begin the actual decorating, she suddenly appears—giggling and excited—ready to help. I don't mind this either. I've decided that whatever it takes to make it fun for both of them is all right with me. What's important is that we're together and they're happy.

I like to keep a pot of stew, chili, or gumbo from my native Louisiana simmering on the stove for a cozy, informal dinner. It's nice to take a break from our work to sit back and admire our accomplishments.

Someday my children will be on their own,

pursuing their individual lives and dreams. That's why I feel it's so important now to create a climate of comfort and joy and lasting memories of Christmas tree trimming that they can look back on with fondness when they're adults.

"He that is of a merry heart hath a continual feast."

Proverbs 15:15

TRADITIONS

C hristmas was coming! Even at seven I knew unmistakably that Christmas was coming because today was tree-trimming day. My parents had made the event into an exciting and joyful family tradition that lasted all afternoon and well into the evening. First, Dad led us deep into the lush Louisiana woods, where we picked out the perfect tree to grace our home. Then, as we approached the front steps bearing our trophy and flushed with the cold and excitement, we were greeted by wonderful aromas from the kitchen. While we had been out tree hunting, Mother had been busy preparing a special dinner for the happy occasion.

While Mom continued her tantalizing work in the kitchen, the rest of us prepared to trim the tree. We retrieved from the attic huge boxes full of our beloved collection of ornaments and strands of colorful lights. Dad began sawing and leveling the tree trunk so it would fit into the stand. My oldest brother, Joey, and I carefully organized the tinsel and glass balls. Trent, our middle brother, had eagerly volunteered for the tedious job of checking each light on the many strands, knowing that if one light were faulty, the whole strand would fail to light.

A STRING OF LIGHTS

We may not have realized it then, but those lights were a perfect symbol of family—connected, each one important, each impacted by the success or failure of the others.

Trent painstakingly laid out each strand of lights along the length of our brand-new wine-colored Naugahyde sofa, meticulously testing each bulb to make sure all were securely in their sockets and in perfect working order.

During the course of our various tasks, Mother called from the kitchen: "Supper is ready and on the table!" We dropped what we were doing and ran to find our places at the dinner table. We all had worked up hearty appetites. As we ate and talked over the events of the day, my dad paused for a moment as if observing something.

"Honey," he asked Mother, "did you leave something on the stove? I smell something burning."

"I don't think I did, but I smell it too," she replied and hurried to the kitchen to check. "There's nothing here," she called.

Instantly one thought struck each of us. The entire family dashed from the table back to the family room, where we had left decorations strewn everywhere. The strands of Christmas lights were just as Trent had left them, shining brightly—burning perfectly symmetrical holes in our beautiful new sofa!

Trent began to howl. He was truly sorry for his careless mistake. Dad quickly stepped to the outlet to unplug the lights while Mother put her arms around Trent to console him. We stood motionless, stunned by the scene that had unfolded. Then we quietly returned to the table to finish our evening meal.

As time went by, we came to accept our sofa with its new characteristics and kept it as a fixture in our home for many years. When friends came to visit and were offered a

seat on our less-than-perfect furniture, we often shared this story with fondness and laughter. Our sofa became a constant reminder of the bonds of love, the inter-connectedness of family, and the rich, family traditions we share during the holiday season and all year long.

"How good and how pleasant it is for brethren to dwell together in unity!"

Psalm 133:1

His Name Is Jesus

Mary, Mary, what's His name
Did you name Him after His father
Or for one of the prophets of old
Whom we cherish and honor
Mary, Mary, tell us again
We have never heard it before
It brings such joy and peace to our hearts
Please won't you tell us once again
His name is Jesus, proclaimed by the angel
His name is Jesus, He is Emmanuel
Hope of the ages, Promised deliverer
His name is Jesus, God with us dwells
Mary, now we know it is true
Not just because you have told us
But for ourselves His love we have felt
And wonderful peace that enfolds us
Mary, still you were chosen of God
To bear the one we adore
Sweet is the name that the angel proclaimed
Please won't you tell us once more

Words and music: Joel and LaBreeska Hemphill

Chicken Gumbo

2 fryer chickens, thoroughly rinsed
1 pound smoked sausage,
   thinly sliced
1 bunch green onions, diced
1 bell pepper, chopped
3 stalks celery, chopped
1 5-ounce package Creole gumbo mix

Vegetable oil, if needed
¼ to ½ cup flour
Salt
Black pepper
Cayenne pepper
3 tablespoons filé (a Cajun spice)
Hot rice

You will also need: Very large pot, Iron skillet, Long-handled spoon

1. In a very large pot, cover the chickens with water and boil them until they're tender and pulling away from the bone. Remove the chickens from the water.
2. Skin and debone the chickens, then place the meat back into the stock. (Steps 1 and 2 can be done the day before and the items stored in the refrigerator.)
3. In an iron skillet, brown the sausage, then drain and reserve the drippings for later. Add the sausage to the stock.
4. Sauté the onions, bell pepper, and celery in half of the sausage drippings. Add these vegetables to the stock.
5. Stir the Creole gumbo mix into the stock.
6. Pour the remaining sausage drippings into the skillet. (Add vegetable oil to the drippings, if needed, to equal ¼ cup.) Add the flour and brown, stirring constantly with long-handled spoon over medium-high heat to make a roux. After 3 or 4 minutes, roux should change in color from cream to a dark red-brown. Remove from heat and add the roux to the stock. Stir well.
7. Add salt, black pepper, and cayenne pepper to taste. Bring the gumbo to a rolling boil, then simmer it for 30 minutes, stirring occasionally.
8. Add 3 tablespoons of filé to the gumbo just before serving, stirring just enough to blend.
9. Serve the gumbo over hot rice. Make it as spicy as you like by adding more cayenne pepper or filé.

Chocolate Chili

3 pounds ground chuck
1 pound pork (any kind), cubed
2 28-ounce cans peeled and diced
  tomatoes
4 cloves garlic, minced
2 teaspoons ground coriander
2 tablespoons all-purpose flour

4 teaspoons ground cumin
4 teaspoons salt
2 large onions, chopped
1 teaspoon ground oregano
6 tablespoons chili powder
4 bay leaves
2 ounces baking semi-sweet chocolate

YOU WILL ALSO NEED: LARGE SKILLET

1. Cook the beef in a large skillet until brown. Add the pork and brown. Drain fat.
2. Stir in the tomatoes, garlic, coriander, flour, cumin, salt, onions, oregano, and chili powder. Cover and simmer for 1 hour.
3. Add the bay leaves, cook for 10 minutes, then remove them. Add the chocolate and stir to combine. Cook 10 minutes more to blend the flavors.

British Tea Bread

1 cup milk

¼ cup sugar

1 teaspoon salt

⅓ cup butter or margarine

½ cup warm water

1 package dry yeast

3 large eggs

4 cups sifted all-purpose flour (sifted before measuring)

1 tablespoon melted butter or margarine

YOU WILL ALSO NEED: SMALL SAUCEPAN; WOODEN SPOON; LARGE BOWL; CANDY THERMOMETER; ELECTRIC MIXER; WAX PAPER; DAMP KITCHEN TOWEL; 10 x 4½-INCH TUBE PAN, GREASED (YOU CAN USE A BUNDT PAN, BUT GREASE AND FLOUR ADEQUATELY, SO CAKE DOESN'T STICK TO PAN.); WIRE RACK

1. In a small pan over medium heat, heat the milk until bubbles form around the edge of the pan. Remove the pan from heat; add sugar, salt, and ⅓ cup butter. Stir with a wooden spoon until the butter is melted. Let this mixture cool at room temperature until it's lukewarm.

2. Pour warm water into a large bowl. (If at all possible, test the temperature of the water; the thermometer should read 120°F.) Sprinkle yeast over the warm water. Let stand about 5 minutes, then stir to dissolve the yeast.

3. When the yeast is completely dissolved, add the lukewarm milk mixture, eggs, and flour. Beat at medium speed for about 2 minutes or until the batter is smooth and no lumps of flour remain. The batter should be bubbly.

4. Cover the bowl with wax paper and then with a damp kitchen towel. Let the batter rise in a warm place free from drafts for about 1 hour or until it has doubled in size.

5. Using a wooden spoon, beat the yeast batter vigorously for 30 seconds.

6. Pour the batter into a greased 10 x 4½-inch tube pan; cover with wax paper and a damp kitchen towel. Let the batter rise in a warm place free from drafts until it has doubled in size, about 45 minutes.

7. In a preheated 350°F oven, bake the bread for 45 minutes or until golden brown. Remove it from the pan to a wire rack. Brush the 1 tablespoon melted butter over the bread. Serve warm. This bread should not be cut with a knife. Instead, split bread into pieces using two forks.

Praline Pumpkin Cake

¾ cup brown sugar
⅓ cup butter or margarine
3 tablespoons whipping cream
1 cup chopped pecans
4 eggs
1⅔ cups granulated sugar
1 cup vegetable oil

1 15-ounce can pumpkin pie
  mix
¼ teaspoon vanilla extract
2 cups all-purpose flour
2 teaspoons baking powder
1 teaspoon baking soda
1 teaspoon salt

Cream-Cheese Filling
1 8-ounce package cream
  cheese, softened
1 cup powdered sugar
1 8-ounce carton whipped
  topping
Chopped pecans

YOU WILL ALSO NEED: SAUCEPAN; 2 9-INCH ROUND CAKE PANS, GREASED; ELECTRIC MIXER; SMALL MIXING BOWL; WOODEN TOOTHPICK; WIRE RACKS; WOODEN SPOON

1. Preheat the oven to 350°F.
2. For topping, cook brown sugar, butter, and whipping cream in saucepan over low heat, stirring until sugar dissolves. Pour into greased cake pans and sprinkle evenly with 1 cup of pecans. Allow to cool.
3. In a large bowl, beat the eggs, granulated sugar, and oil at medium speed of mixer. Add the pumpkin pie mix and vanilla and beat well.
4. Combine the remaining ingredients in small bowl and add them to the pumpkin mixture, beating until blended. Spoon the batter evenly into the cake pans.
5. Bake the cake layers at 350°F for 30 to 35 minutes or until a wooden pick inserted in the center comes out clean. Cool the cake layers in the pans on wire racks for 5 minutes; then remove the layers from the pans and cool them on wire racks.

Cream-Cheese Filling

1. Whip the cream cheese in small bowl at medium speed of mixer until creamy. Mixing at low speed, add the powdered sugar and mix until completely blended, about 2 minutes. Fold whipped topping into the cream-cheese mixture with a wooden spoon.
2. Place one cake layer on a serving plate, praline side up, and spread evenly with the cream-cheese filling. Add the second cake layer, praline side up, and top with the remaining filling. Sprinkle the cake with chopped pecans. Store in refrigerator.

Oatmeal Cake

PICTURED ON PAGE 10

1½ cups boiling water
1 cup quick oats
½ cup (1 stick) butter or margarine, softened
1 cup brown sugar
1 cup granulated sugar
2 eggs
1½ cups sifted flour
½ teaspoon salt
1 teaspoon each, cinnamon, nutmeg, and baking soda

Topping

¼ cup brown sugar
½ cup granulated sugar
1 cup coconut
1 cup chopped nuts
6 tablespoons butter or margarine
¼ cup light cream
¼ teaspoon vanilla

YOU WILL ALSO NEED: ELECTRIC MIXER; 9 x 13-INCH BAKING PAN, GREASED; TWO MEDIUM BOWLS; SAUCEPAN

1. Preheat the oven to 350°F.
2. Pour boiling water over the oats and mix well.
3. Cream together butter, brown sugar, and granulated sugar. Mixture will be somewhat grainy. Beat in the eggs, then stir in the soaked oatmeal.
4. In a separate bowl, stir together flour, salt, cinnamon, nutmeg, and baking soda. Add to the oatmeal mixture and beat with electric mixer on low.
5. Turn the batter into the greased pan and bake for 30 to 35 minutes. Cool the cake in the pan.

Topping

1. Combine all ingredients in a saucepan, except the vanilla. Heat until bubbly, remove from heat, and add vanilla.
2. Pour the topping onto the cake.

Old-Fashioned Vegetable-Beef Soup

⅛ cup salad oil
1 medium onion, diced
2 celery stalks, sliced
3 medium carrots, sliced
½ head cabbage, shredded
1½ pounds beef for stew, cut into
   ½-inch chunks
2 14-ounce cans chicken broth
6 medium potatoes, peeled

1 28-ounce can stewed tomatoes,
   chopped
6 cups water
1 16-ounce can whole kernel corn
1 8-ounce can baby lima beans, drained
4 teaspoons salt
½ teaspoon pepper
1½ teaspoons basil

You will also need: Stew pot, Slotted spoon, Medium bowl

1. In stew pot, sauté the onion, celery, carrots, and cabbage in salad oil over medium heat until the vegetables are lightly browned, stirring frequently. With a slotted spoon, remove the vegetables to medium bowl and set them aside. (Do not drain oil.)
2. In the same pot, cook the beef chunks in the remaining oil over high heat, stirring frequently, until the meat is well browned.
3. Add two cans of chicken broth.
4. Shred 1 potato and cut the remaining 5 potatoes into 1-inch cubes. To the meat chunks, add the reserved vegetable mixture, potatoes, tomatoes with their liquid, and the remaining ingredients. Bring these to a rapid boil. Reduce the heat to low; cover and simmer for 25 to 30 minutes, or just until the beef chunks and potato cubes are tender. If the soup becomes too thick, add water or broth.

LAGNIAPPE

Several centuries ago, French immigrants came to Louisiana and adopted it as their home. Growing up in Louisiana, I enjoyed the benefits of their wonderful cultural contributions of music, spices, and recipes, known as "Cajun."

The Cajun people are also known for their generosity and hospitality. Often Cajun merchants would throw in a little extra, for free, with what you bought. This is known as the "lagniappe" (pronounced "lan-yap"). *Lagniappe* is a French word meaning "something extra," similar to the idea of a baker's dozen.

In each chapter of this book, I've included a lagniappe—extra ideas or crafts for you to try. Enjoy!

- Assemble the tree (if artificial) and string the lights before calling the kids. They'll get more enjoyment out of decorating if they don't have to wait while the adults do the hard part.

- Decorate your own wreath this year with things that represent your family. Items relating to sports, job, schools, or other hobbies make fun additions.

- In addition to your "decorator" tree, put up at least one tree on which kids can hang decorations they make.

- Having "dinner on the grounds" is a fun way to start the tree decorating process—a picnic in your family room, right in the middle of the decorations!

CHRISTMAS TREE ORNAMENTS
PICTURED BELOW AND ON PAGE 10

YOU WILL NEED:

Newspaper (or something to protect work surface)

Paper-mâché ornament (from a craft store)

Gold spray paint (or color of your choice)

Favorite picture of your child
(or any favorite picture)

Glue or glue stick

Pencil

Stencil pattern (optional)

Ruler (optional)

Fine-point tube of fabric
paint (color of your choice)

Extra-fine glitter

Crystal stones (optional)

Superglue (optional)

Ribbon

Hot glue gun

1. Spray-paint paper-mâché ornament on well-covered surface and allow to dry.
2. Paste photo in the center, if desired.
3. With a pencil, draw the desired design. You can draw the design freehand or use a ruler or stenciled pattern.
4. With tube of fabric paint, paint along penciled lines. While paint is still wet, sprinkle with glitter; allow to dry.
5. Set crystal stones with superglue, if desired.
6. Tie a bow around the ornament loop. Glue bow in place with hot glue gun.

Christmas Is

CHRISTMAS IS FOR KIDS

Santa and sleigh bells, bicycles and baby dolls, programs and parties—Christmas is for kids! While Santa and his elves are busy making toys for good girls and boys, children everywhere are visiting malls for a glance at the little old man with a fluffy, white beard and funny glasses. Elaborate explanations are made up for why Santa seems to be everywhere and how he knows what every child wants. That's the magic and make-believe part of Christmas. But the true meaning of Christmas is revealed through children who don shepherds' costumes and quote scriptures about the birth of a baby who changed history forever. On Christmas, parents flock to churches where kids are center-stage— their children portray the story of another child who came to be our Savior.

19

HEARTH, HOME, AND HELPING HANDS

For many years I have found great joy in giving handmade, delectable treats as Christmas gifts. It's wonderfully rewarding to see the recipients' delight as they bite into the festive fare.

This precious holiday tradition was handed down to me from my mother, who, for as long as I can remember, has taken great pride in it. From the time I was a small child, I've watched her spend countless days in the kitchen each holiday season, baking scrumptious fruitcakes to give as gifts to her family and dearest friends.

She took great pains to find the freshest nutmeats, coconut, and candied fruits, then mixed them all together to make the "perfect" treats. The aromas wafting from the oven and throughout our home made the mouths of our family and guests water, and made a lasting impression on me.

My mother graciously allowed me to help her in the kitchen; she is a master at decorating baked goods, and she was eager to share with me her "tricks of the trade." She taught me the importance of presentation—to "tickle the eyes" as well as the taste buds. She was patient, ignoring my mistakes as an apprentice and always cutting the first cake for me to sample.

Those times spent in the kitchen with my mother have left me with many pleasurable memories as well as the desire to share the joys of this tradition with my own children. I try to include them wherever they show interest, and I always allow their little hands to work alongside mine—especially when I'm making candy or cookies.

I see much of myself in them and relive sweet holidays from my youth as I watch them work. I try hard to be as gracious to my little apprentices as my mother was to me.

I've also started a new tradition. When my daughter was three years old, I began buying her a place setting of china each year for Christmas. Inside each box, I include a letter recounting the highlights of her life during the past twelve months. My plan is to present this special gift to Jasmine when she gets married. When she opens the packages, she'll find not only enough china for many guests as she continues the tradition of hospitality, but also a sentimental record of her childhood.

In our hectic society, where many work hard just to support their families and make ends meet, I understand how difficult it is to find time and energy to do everything we'd like. But some things are too important to neglect. I believe the kitchen

is the heart of the home, where family relationships are bonded in fellowship. Whether preparing or just sharing meals together, memories are made, and rewards will be tasted and treasured for generations to come.

"Children are an heritage of the LORD: and the fruit of the womb is his reward. As arrows are in the hand of a mighty man; so are children of the youth. Happy is the man that hath his quiver full of them."

Psalm 127:3–5

TRADITIONS

DADDY'S DETOUR

The Christmas Eve excitement of a five-year-old child can barely be contained, and I was no exception. Our entire family was dressed in our holiday best and busy getting ready for the trip to Grandma's, where we would reunite with beloved family members who had traveled from various parts of the country. We kids scurried to help Dad carry the beautifully wrapped packages from under the Christmas tree to the trunk of the car. He carefully arranged them so as not to disturb the scrumptious dishes my mother had spent most of the day preparing.

Once the car was loaded and every detail attended, we settled into our green, 1963 Buick. My parents were in the front seat, and my two brothers sat with me in the back. Our hearts pounded with excitement. We chattered nervously and kept our eyes riveted to the road ahead, watching anxiously for the moment when my grandparents' front porch light would come into view and the festivities would begin.

Because we made this trip often, I knew every stop and every curve along the thirty-mile route. Before long my brothers and I realized that we had veered from our usual course and were in an unfamiliar area of town.

"Where are we going?" "I thought we were going to Grandma's house!" "Won't we be late?" we clamored.

"Did I forget to mention that I had to run an errand on the way?" Dad replied.

Our spirits plummeted, and I was incensed. But I knew I could complain a good deal more with my dad out of earshot, so I waited until we came to a stop and he disappeared inside the building. I swiftly began airing my complaints: "Why couldn't Dad run errands another day?" "Doesn't he care that all of our family is waiting for us, or that Christmas dinner may begin without us?" I had even worked up a few crocodile tears to add gravity to my case.

Fifteen minutes passed…twenty…finally Dad emerged from the store with an enormous box in his hands. He carried it carefully to the car and opened the back door, where I was seated. "Merry Christmas, darling," he said with a sweet smile as he gently laid the parcel in my lap.

I was stunned. Without a word, I lifted the lid from the box. There inside was the most beautiful, life-size baby doll I had ever seen. She was dressed in a delicate white christening gown embroidered with tiny pink rosettes and a matching bonnet. Beneath her beautiful skirt she wore white stockings and little satin slippers that laced at the ankle. She looked up at me with an expression on her tiny face that was simply angelic.

I was ashamed. I knew I had acted badly, and I began to cry. But these tears were unlike the ones I had shed earlier in anger and self-pity. These were tears of remorse. I threw my arms around my dad's neck and kissed his kind, loving face.

Many times in my life, I've looked back on this event and realized that I'm still learning the same lesson, only on a larger scale. Many times my impatience has caused me

needless pain while I fretted and complained, not seeing the hand of my heavenly Father doing something wonderful on my behalf. But I'm learning to trust that even when I think things have gotten off course, He loves me and will work out everything for my good (see Romans 8:28).

"But let patience have her perfect work, that ye may be perfect and entire, wanting nothing."

James 1:4

Christmas Is for Kids

Do you long for Christmases the way they used to be
That filled up all your senses with love and lighted trees
You can know the thrill again, I'll tell you where to start
Christmas joy is for the young and the young at heart
Christmas is for kids
Jingle bells and mistletoe
And snow rides on our sleds
There's a feeling in the air
God's love is everywhere
Open up your heart
And let the season take you back
To yesterday and you'll be glad you did
When you start to feel that yuletide feeling
You're a kid again
And Christmas is for kids

Holiday Sugar Cookies

2½ cups flour
1½ teaspoons baking powder
Pinch of salt
1 cup (2 sticks) butter or margarine,
    softened
1¼ cups sugar

2 eggs
1 teaspoon almond extract
½ teaspoon nutmeg
Canned frosting (optional)
Sprinkles (optional)

YOU WILL ALSO NEED: Large bowl; Electric mixer; Wax paper; Cutting board, lightly floured; Rolling pin; Cookie cutters; Cookie sheet, lightly greased

1. Preheat the oven to 400°F.
2. Measure all ingredients (except frosting and sprinkles) into large bowl. Beat at medium speed until well mixed, occasionally scraping the sides of the bowl.
3. Shape the dough into a ball. Wrap it with wax paper and refrigerate for 2 to 3 hours, until dough is easy to handle.
4. On a lightly floured cutting board, roll out half of the dough at a time, keeping the rest refrigerated. For crisp cookies, roll paper thin; for softer cookies, roll to ¼-inch thickness.
5. With floured cookie cutters, cut the dough into various shapes. Roll the dough trimmings and continue to cut shapes.
6. Place the cookies on a greased cookie sheet, spaced ½ inch apart.
7. Bake for 6 minutes until "golden" brown around the edges.
8. Serve plain or ice with canned frosting and a variety of sprinkles.

Chocolate Mice

MAKES 12; PICTURED ON PAGE 26

12 Maraschino cherries, with stems (for bodies and tails of mice)

6 ounces semisweet chocolate morsels, melted

12 chocolate-covered graham crackers

12 Hershey's Kisses (for heads and noses of mice)

24 almond slices

YOU WILL ALSO NEED: PAPER TOWELS, MICROWAVE OVEN, GLASS BOWL, RED DECORATING GEL

1. Drain the cherries and pat them completely dry with paper towels.
2. Melt chocolate morsels in microwave 1 minute on high. Stir. Continue melting 30 seconds at a time, stirring between each 30 seconds so that chocolate does not caramelize.
3. Holding a cherry by the stem, dredge the cherry through the melted chocolate and place it on half of a graham cracker, stem pointing outward.
4. Dredge the bottom of a Hershey's Kiss through the chocolate coating and place it in front of the cherry. The melted chocolate will act as a type of glue, holding the Kiss in place.
5. Dip the narrow end of an almond slice in the melted chocolate and press it to the flat side of the Kiss to make an ear. Repeat for the other side.
6. With the decorating gel, place dots for the eyes and nose.

CANDY'S NOTE: "'Twas the night before Christmas, when all through the house, not a creature was stirring, not even a…" These chocolate mice are fun for kids to make and are a perfect complement to Clement C. Moore's classic tale.

Grandmother Christmas's Cookies

MAKES 9 DOZEN; PICTURED ON PAGE 26

2½ cups oatmeal
1 cup (2 sticks) butter or margarine
1 cup sugar
1 cup brown sugar
2 eggs
1 teaspoon vanilla

2 cups flour
1 teaspoon baking powder
1 teaspoon baking soda
12 ounces semisweet chocolate morsels
1 4-ounce chocolate bar, grated
1½ cups chopped nuts

YOU WILL ALSO NEED: FOOD PROCESSOR OR BLENDER; ELECTRIC MIXER; LARGE BOWL; SMALL BOWL; COOKIE SHEET, GREASED

1. Preheat the oven to 400°F.
2. In a food processor or blender, grind oatmeal to a fine powder and set aside.
3. Cream together butter and sugars in large bowl until fluffy. Mixing at low speed, add eggs and vanilla.
4. In a small bowl, sift together flour, baking powder, and baking soda.
5. Alternately add the flour mixture and oatmeal to the butter mixture, blending well after each addition.
6. Fold remaining ingredients into the dough and drop by spoonfuls onto a greased cookie sheet.
7. Bake for 8 to 10 minutes or until the cookies are lightly golden.

Christmas Tree Cookie Centerpiece

PICTURED ON PAGE 26

3 12-ounce packages chocolate morsels

Pirouette cookies, 6 to 8 5½-ounce packages

1 12-ounce package white chocolate morsels to
   drizzle on "tree" (optional)

6 ounces pecan halves

Red and green candied cherries or gumdrops

YOU WILL ALSO NEED: DOUBLE BOILER, STYROFOAM CONE (4-INCH BASE, 9 INCHES HIGH), 14-INCH PLATTER OR CAKE BOARD, BOW AND SMALL ORNAMENT (OPTIONAL)

1. In the top of a double boiler, melt the chocolate morsels over warm—not boiling—water.

2. Spread a little of the melted morsels on the bottom of the cone, and anchor this in the center of the platter or cake board.

3. Lightly coat the cone with the melted chocolate morsels. Arrange pirouette cookies in a starburst pattern around base of the cone (see photo on page 26), using the melted morsels as "glue."

4. Layer rows of cookies, encircling the cone and reducing the number of cookies with each row as you move up the cone. Trim and shorten some cookies, if necessary, to properly shape the tree. Build 6 to 8 rows in this fashion. As you approach the top of the cone, stack the cookies in teepee fashion (see photo).

5. Drizzle over all with the melted chocolate morsels. If desired, also drizzle with melted white chocolate morsels.

6. Sandwich pecan halves together with the melted chocolate morsels to make "pine cones." Attach these to the tree with a little of the melted morsels. Trim the tree with candied red and green cherries or gumdrops. If desired, place a bow and a small ornament at the top.

Peanut Butter Balls

MAKES 150 BALLS; PICTURED ON PAGE 26

1 cup (2 sticks) butter or margarine, softened

2 boxes (about 2 pounds) powdered sugar

32 ounces crunchy peanut butter

1 cup ground pecans

15 ounces semisweet chocolate morsels

1 4-ounce block paraffin wax (This usually can be found with the canning supplies in your grocery store.)

YOU WILL ALSO NEED: LARGE BOWL, ELECTRIC MIXER, DOUBLE BOILER, TOOTHPICKS, WAX PAPER

1. In a large bowl, mix together butter, powdered sugar, peanut butter, and pecans. Roll into balls 1 inch in diameter. Chill until firm.
2. In a double boiler, melt the chocolate morsels and paraffin, being careful not to bring the water beneath the morsels to a boil. Keep the chocolate in the double boiler over low heat while dipping balls. Periodically remove the double boiler from heat if necessary.
3. Coat peanut butter balls by inserting a toothpick into each and then dipping them into the chocolate. Place them on wax paper to set.

CANDY'S NOTE: This recipe calls for 2 sticks of butter, but to really bring out the peanut butter flavor, try using only 1 stick.

Snowman S'mores
PICTURED ON PAGE 26

Ingredients for each s'more

3 ounces white chocolate morsels
2 pretzel sticks
½ of a 1.55-ounce Hershey milk chocolate bar

½ graham cracker
2 marshmallows
Orange decorating gel
Black decorating gel

YOU WILL ALSO NEED: MICROWAVE OVEN, GLASS BOWL, MICROWAVEABLE PLATE,
WAX PAPER, SHARP KITCHEN TOOL

1. In a glass bowl, melt the white chocolate morsels in a microwave oven on high for 1 minute. Stir. Continue melting 30 seconds at a time stirring between each 30 seconds so that white chocolate doesn't caramelize.
2. Dip pretzel sticks in the melted morsels, place them on wax paper, and lay them aside to set.
3. Place the chocolate candy bar on the graham cracker. Place the graham cracker on a microwaveable plate. Microwave for 10 seconds, just long enough to adhere the chocolate to the cracker but still keep its shape.
4. Using melted white morsels as "glue," stack marshmallows on top of the chocolate candy bar to form the body of the snowman.
5. With a sharp kitchen tool, pierce the sides of the bottom marshmallow and insert the pretzels for arms.
6. Make dots with orange (for nose) and black (for eyes and mouth) decorating gel.
7. Sit back and watch your youngsters enjoy!

- Cut the sandwiches you pack in children's school lunches with Christmas cookie cutters. This will surely brighten their day!

- Host a cookie decorating party with the neighborhood kids. Bake cookies beforehand so they can get right to the decorating fun.

- When making Christmas cookies, be sure to make plenty. Then you can have them on hand when guests drop by. Or send some to school with your children for teachers—your little chefs will give and receive lots of holiday cheer!

- Forget cooking! Take your kids to their favorite restaurant and then drive around, looking at Christmas lights.

- Don't let Christmas pass by without helping your kids experience the gift of giving. Taking cookies to a nursing home, an elderly friend, or a sick child will help teach this valuable lesson.

- Start a Christmas scrapbook. Keep it on a table in the family room and add new pages as the holiday season progresses.

BOOK BAG OR APRON

YOU WILL NEED:
Book bag or apron (from a craft store)
Straight pins
Cardboard
Stencil (your choice)
Fabric paint (color of your choice)
Fine-point tube of glittered fabric paint
Extra fine glitter
Paint sponge
Crystal stones (optional)
Superglue

1. Pin stencil to desired area. Place cardboard inside bag or under apron (in case the paint bleeds through).
2. With a paint sponge, dab paint over stencil. Remove the stencil and allow paint to dry.
3. Trace the edges with glittered fabric paint. Sprinkle on glitter while this is still wet.
4. Glue on crystal stones, if desired.

CANDY'S NOTE: I like making these for schoolteachers or Sunday school teachers. I never know what to buy for them, and these are things they can definitely use!

- Use every opportunity to teach your children about Jesus. For instance, the twinkling lights on each house should remind us of the single star that welcomed His birth. A stay in a hotel is an occasion to talk about the fact that there was no room in the inn for Him. A freshly cut tree can spark a discussion about Jesus' being hung on the cross (once a tree).

Christmas

CHRISTMAS
PARTIES

This is the time of the year to be extravagant! Not with things, but with people. Splurge on friends and family. Load up on fellowship and hugs. Wear green and red, and put out your finest china. Or use paper plates printed with festively decorated Christmas trees. Get together with those you hold dear and draw them close as you remember together that Christmas is for celebrating.

It's party time! Come on over!

CELEBRATE!

Is anything more fun during the holidays than a Christmas party? There's something wonderful about getting all dressed up in dazzling holiday attire to share an evening with friends.

Because my travels often take me away from home, I've become more selective in accepting invitations as my time at home has become more precious. This has helped me develop entertaining skills I probably wouldn't have explored otherwise. Inviting friends to our home has become a thrilling challenge to me. From intimate dinners to large, elaborate gatherings, I love to allow my imagination freedom to create various holiday celebrations.

I have come to the conclusion that even God must love Christmas parties. After all, the concept was His, and He developed the prototype. On the very first Christmas, He hosted a gala beyond imagination. He sent invitations ("I bring you good tidings of great joy," Luke 2:10) to a diverse group of people ("which shall be to

all people" Luke 2:10). A spectacular light display ("The glory of the Lord shone round about them" Luke 2:9) and a choir of heavenly angels ("There was with the angel a multitude of the heavenly host praising God, and saying, Glory to God in the highest" Luke 2:13–14) entertained and amazed His guests. What an extravaganza!

Did you know that Jesus' first miracle was performed at a party (see John 2), and one of the last things He did before He was betrayed and crucified was to host a dinner party for His dearest friends (see John 13:1–5)? God smiles when His children fellowship together.

On occasions when my husband and I are able to step out for parties during the holidays, we enjoy having time away from the children to enjoy each other. We like making new friends and enriching relationships as we enjoy the festive Christmas season.

"Whether therefore ye eat, or drink, or whatsoever ye do, do all to the glory of God."

1 Corinthians 10:31

CHRISTMAS CAROLING

One year during the Christmas season, I was planning a dinner party for many of my gospel music friends. I happened to see an old acquaintance, then president of Baptist Hospital in Nashville, Tennessee, and asked if he and his wife would like to attend. His immediate response to my invitation was this: "During the course of that evening, is there any way you and your singing guests could come to the hospital? It would be grand for you all to carol through the halls. Our patients would so appreciate it." This was an idea I had not entertained, but knowing the benevolent hearts of my friends, I was sure they would be more than willing. I immediately said, "Yes."

On the evening of the party, soon after the guests arrived at my home, we boarded a Silver Eagle bus and eagerly headed for the hospital. The bus rolled up to the hospital entrance and we filed out one by one. We were completely surprised by the reception we received. The hospital president and his staff greeted us with smiles and open arms. The local television stations had heard of our mission of mercy and were standing poised with camera equipment in hand to chronicle the event for the evening news.

Yet, amid the fanfare, our hearts were heavy for the hurting. We were anxious to allow the Holy Spirit to work through us, so up the elevator we went. Corridor after corridor, door to door, we shared the message of Jesus and His birth, wishing "peace on earth, good will toward men" to every patient, each family, and even the nursing staff.

At times tears flowed; at other times we rejoiced, yielding ourselves to be instruments of healing, bringing cheer and hope to those we met. My mind's eye can still vividly see one particular elderly gentleman. As we sang to him, he motioned for his wife to help him stand. Pajama-clad, his cheeks wet with tears, the man joined in singing with all his might: "Glory to God, all glory in the highest; O come, let us adore Him."

This Christmas party won't soon be forgotten, because it deeply impacted the hearts of some gospel singers who set out merely to do a simple good deed. Our spreading goodwill gave us a feeling of goodwill in return, and we were blessed beyond measure.

"Glory to God in the highest, and on earth peace, good will toward men."

Luke 2:14

Shepherd's Song

I reclined in my easy chair; I decided to take a break
After a day of Christmas shopping and before I bake a cake.
The Christmas tree's assembled, standing naked in the den,
I know I'll trim it later, but I really can't say when.
My mind numbers my chores, things I must get done,
Like lambs leaping through a gate, I count them one by one.
Just a moment to close my eyes…I feel quite overwhelmed…
Floating, drifting, am I dreaming? Hey! This looks like Bethlehem!
I'm not lying in my easy chair but on a grassy knoll;
The sheep that I've been counting are those I'm tending in a fold.
Do I hear singing? What radiant light!
I feel the brush of snowy wings—I see angels in the night!
They lift their voices in a glorious song and point toward an Inn:
"Yonder is a King, a Savior for all Men!"
Why tell a simple shepherd? Do they sense my soul's thirst?
With all my strength I begin to run, that I might see Him first.
As I reach my destination, I find no dwelling for a King,

Just a lowly stable beneath a star's brightest beam.
A force I can't withstand draws me through the door
To view a wondrous scene like none beheld before
Three noble men from the east, bearing frankincense and gold
And there, a shepherd holds a lamb, near a burrow and her foal.
I gaze upon a manger and a young girl kneeling low,
Who embodies the essence of innocence. Her face is all aglow.
I was feeling like an intruder until she looked at me and smiled;
Then she nodded as if to say, "Have you looked upon the child?"
My eyes fell on a babe in rags, lying peaceful and so sweet.
My soul cries out, "He's the Son of God!" I fall to worship at His feet.
As I behold His glory, my sin and sorrow roll away.
I find all I've been searching for sleeping on the hay.
Such love I never knew could be; as God pours out His grace,
Floods of joy overflow my heart, and tears spill down my face.
Silence is abruptly broken as bells begin to chime.
Suddenly, against my will, I'm carried to another time.
My computer comes into focus; the phone is ringing on the wall.
"Take me back to the Christ Child!" my voice begins to call.
I stop myself in reverence; a holy presence I sense is near.
"Jesus isn't in a manger, He is really here!"
"In a dream I've been changed," I can't help but shout;
I have found what the Christmas spirit is really all about.
It isn't gifts under tinseled trees or pretty cards in the mail;
But it's Jesus Christ, God with us, who is Emmanuel.

CANDY CHRISTMAS

Savory Artichoke Cheese Hors D'oeuvre

MAKES 10 TO 12 SERVINGS; PICTURED ON PAGE 42

¼ cup fine, dry-seasoned bread crumbs

2 8-ounce packages cream cheese, softened

¾ cup crumbled feta cheese

1 cup sour cream

3 large eggs

1 9-ounce package frozen artichoke hearts, thawed, divided

½ cup sliced scallions

1 clove garlic, minced

⅛ teaspoon tarragon

1 teaspoon dried basil leaves, crushed

Fresh basil leaves

Red pepper, cut into thin strips

YOU WILL ALSO NEED: 9-INCH SPRINGFORM PAN, GENEROUSLY GREASED; LARGE BOWL; PAPER TOWELS; ELECTRIC MIXER; KNIFE; RUBBER SPATULA; WIRE RACK

1. Preheat the oven to 375°F.
2. Sprinkle inside of pan with breadcrumbs to coat. Tap pan to remove excess crumbs; reserve excess crumbs. Set pan aside.
3. In a large bowl, at medium-high speed, beat cream cheese until light and fluffy, scraping bowl frequently. Add feta cheese, sour cream, and eggs; beat until mixture is blended and very smooth.
4. Remove excess moisture from artichoke hearts patting with paper towels; reserve 2 or 3 for a garnish.
5. Finely chop artichoke hearts (except those reserved for garnish). (Hint: a French chef's knife works best.) Add to cheese mixture.
6. Add scallions, garlic, tarragon, and basil to the cheese mixture.
7. Spoon cheese mixture into prepared pan, spreading evenly with rubber spatula, being careful not to disturb breadcrumbs.
8. Bake for 35 minutes or until puffed and golden brown. Remove from oven and place on wire rack. Cool to room temperature.
9. Cover top of pan with plastic wrap; don't let it touch surface of hors d'oeuvre. Refrigerate for 3 hours or overnight.
10. Cook reserved artichoke hearts as package label directs.
11. Remove side of springform pan. Pat reserved breadcrumbs onto side of hors d'oeuvre. Garnish with fresh basil leaves, red pepper strips, and cooked artichoke hearts. Slice hors d'oeuvre into wedges.

Five-Pound Fudge

PICTURED ON PAGE 42

1 13-ounce jar marshmallow crème
18 ounces semisweet chocolate morsels
4 cups pecans, chopped
4 cups sugar
½ cup (1 stick) butter or margarine
1 12-ounce can evaporated milk
Pinch of salt

YOU WILL ALSO NEED: MEDIUM BOWL, HEAVY SAUCEPAN, WAX PAPER OR LARGE PANS

1. Mix together marshmallow crème, chocolate morsels, and pecans in medium bowl; set aside.
2. Combine sugar, butter, evaporated milk, and salt in a heavy saucepan. Bring to a boil, stirring constantly (it scorches easily). Lower heat, but maintain boil for 8 minutes, still stirring constantly.
3. Immediately add marshmallow mixture to the cooked mixture. Blend well and set out by tablespoonfuls on wax paper or pour into large pans and cut when cool.

CANDY'S NOTE: If you're using the spooning technique, it helps to have assistance for this part of the process. There's a lot of fudge, and it cools very quickly. This recipe freezes well.

Candy's Wonderful Caramels

MAKES 4 DOZEN; PICTURED ON PAGE 42

2 cups light corn syrup
1 14-ounce can sweetened, condensed milk
1 cup (2 sticks) butter or margarine
4 cups sugar
1 cup whipping cream
1½ cups milk
2 teaspoons vanilla
2 cups nuts
Semisweet chocolate morsels (optional)

YOU WILL ALSO NEED: 9 x 13-INCH BAKING PAN, GREASED; 6-QUART DUTCH OVEN; WOODEN SPOON; PASTRY BRUSH; CANDY THERMOMETER; WAX PAPER

1. In a Dutch oven, mix corn syrup; sweetened, condensed milk; butter; sugar; whipping cream; and milk over medium heat. Stir occasionally with a wooden spoon until the mixture comes to a boil. If sugar crystals are present, wash down the sides of the pan with a wet pastry brush. Clip a candy thermometer to the side of the pan. Cook the mixture, stirring constantly, until it reaches 240°F or soft-ball stage.
2. Remove from heat and stir in vanilla and nuts.
3. Pour, without scraping, into the prepared pan. Allow to stand at room temperature overnight.
4. Cut into 1-inch squares. Wrap in wax paper or dip in melted semisweet chocolate morsels.

Christmas Cheese Ball

PICTURED ON PAGE 42

2 8-ounce packages cream cheese, softened
2 cups (8 ounces) sharp cheddar cheese, grated
1 tablespoon onion, finely chopped
1 tablespoon pimientos, diced
1 tablespoon green pepper, diced
2 teaspoons Worcestershire sauce
1 teaspoon lemon juice
Chopped pecans, toasted

YOU WILL ALSO NEED: COOKIE SHEET, UNGREASED; LARGE BOWL

1. Preheat oven to 350°F.
2. Combine all ingredients except pecans in large bowl; mix well.
3. Spread pecans in a single layer on an ungreased cookie sheet. Bake 4 to 5 minutes, stirring occasionally, until pecans are golden brown.
4. Shape the mixture into two balls and roll each ball in the pecans.
5. Cover and chill. Remove from the refrigerator 15 minutes before serving.
6. Serve with crackers.

Mexican Bean Dip

MAKES 8 TO 10 SERVINGS

1 8-ounce package cream cheese, softened
8 ounces sour cream
1 package dry taco seasoning
1 15-ounce can refried beans
1 cup salsa, drained
2 cups taco-flavored grated cheddar cheese, divided

YOU WILL ALSO NEED: ELECTRIC MIXER, 9 X 12-INCH OVEN-SAFE DISH OR CHAFING DISH

1. Preheat the oven to 350°F.
2. Cream softened cream cheese until smooth; add sour cream and taco seasoning. Fold in refried beans, salsa, and 1 cup of cheddar cheese.
3. Pour the mixture into the dish and sprinkle remaining cheese on top. Bake at 350°F for 35 minutes or until cheese is melted and lightly browned.
4. Serve with tortilla chips and guacamole if desired.

CANDY'S NOTE: This recipe was given to me by my sweet sister-in-law and wonderful friend, Bethni Hemphill.

Triple-Chocolate Decadence Cake

PICTURED ON PAGE 42

⅓ cup half-and-half

2 1-ounce squares unsweetened chocolate, finely
   chopped

⅔ cup shortening

1¾ cups sugar

3 large eggs

2½ cups all-purpose flour

1 teaspoon baking soda

½ teaspoon salt

1 cup buttermilk

1 teaspoon vanilla extract

Frosting

24 ounces semisweet chocolate morsels

1 quart heavy cream

1 teaspoon vanilla

3 cups powdered sugar, sifted

Trees

½ pound green "chocolate"
   candy (from craft store or
   cooking supply store)

White and red "chocolate"
   candy for decorating
   (optional)

YOU WILL ALSO NEED: 3 9-INCH ROUND CAKE PANS, WAX PAPER, 2-QUART SAUCEPAN, ELECTRIC MIXER, LARGE BOWL, WOODEN TOOTHPICK, WIRE RACKS, WIRE WHISK, MICROWAVE, GLASS BOWL, PLASTIC SQUEEZE BOTTLE FOR SQUEEZING MELTED CHOCOLATE (THIS LOOKS LIKE A CONDIMENT BOTTLE AND CAN BE PURCHASED FROM A CRAFT STORE OR COOKING SUPPLY STORE.), WAX PAPER

1. Preheat the oven to 350°F. Line cake pans with wax paper. Grease and flour the wax paper and set the pans aside.

2. Bring the half-and-half to a simmer over medium heat. Remove from heat and add unsweetened chocolate. Let stand for 1 minute. Stir gently until chocolate melts completely. Cool to room temperature.

3. Beat the shortening at medium speed until fluffy. Gradually add sugar and the chocolate mixture, beating at medium speed for 5 to 7 minutes. Add eggs, one at a time, beating after each addition.

4. Combine flour, soda, and salt. Add this to the shortening mixture alternately with buttermilk, beginning and ending with the flour mixture. Mix at low speed after each addition until blended. Mix in the vanilla.

5. Pour the batter into the prepared pans. Bake at 350°F for 20 minutes or until a wooden pick inserted in the center comes out mostly clean. Cool the cake layers in pans on wire racks for 10 minutes. Remove the layers from the pans and peel off the wax paper. Cool the cake layers completely on wire racks.

Frosting

1. In a 2-quart saucepan, combine the semisweet chocolate morsels and heavy cream. Simmer over low heat, stirring constantly, until the mixture begins to bubble (about 30 minutes). Remove from heat.
2. With a wire whisk, stir in vanilla and powdered sugar. Continue stirring until well blended and the mixture is smooth. Chill for 2 to 3 hours in a refrigerator until the mixture is of spreading consistency. Spread frosting over the cooled cake.

Trees

1. In a glass bowl, melt green "chocolate" candy in microwave 1 minute on high. Stir. Continue melting 30 seconds at a time, stirring between each 30 seconds so that candy does not caramelize.
2. Pour melted green "chocolate" candy into plastic squeeze bottle.
3. On wax paper, squeeze out candy in the shapes of trees. To do this, draw an upside-down, narrow V with the candy. Still "drawing" with the candy, trace along the outside of that shape, making another, wider upside-down V. Repeat a third time to complete the shape of a tree.
4. Draw a candy trunk about 2 inches long (enough to hold the tree firmly upright in the cake) at the bottom of the tree. Decorate trees with melted white and red candy if desired.
5. Allow the trees to set for about 10 minutes. When hardened, lift them from the wax paper and press into the top of the cake so the trees stand upright.

Russian Tea Mix

PICTURED ON PAGE 42

½ cup instant tea

2½ cups sugar

2 scant cups Tang

2 5-ounce packages lemonade mix (with sugar)

2 teaspoons cinnamon

1 teaspoon cloves

YOU WILL ALSO NEED: AIRTIGHT CONTAINER (TO HOLD 6 CUPS) OR 6 1-CUP DECORATIVE JARS FOR GIFT GIVING (SEE PHOTO ON PAGE 42)

1. Mix together all ingredients and store in a jar.
2. To serve, add two teaspoons to one cup hot water.

Almond Roca

PICTURED ON PAGE 42

2 cups almonds, chopped and divided

2 cups (4 sticks) butter or margarine

2 cups sugar

6 1.55-ounce small Hershey milk chocolate bars

8 ounces semisweet chocolate morsels

YOU WILL ALSO NEED: BAKING SHEET, LIGHTLY GREASED; SAUCEPAN; LARGE KNIFE

1. Spread the almonds in the bottom of a lightly greased cookie sheet, saving about ½ cup for the finishing touch.
2. Melt butter in a sauce pan, add sugar, and stir constantly until the mixture is the color of peanut butter. Pour over the almonds.
3. Unwrap candy bars and place them on top of the hot mixture. Sprinkle with semisweet morsels. As the chocolate melts, spread it evenly over the candy mixture. Score the candy into serving sizes while it's still warm.
4. Top with remaining almonds and allow to set. When the candy is hard, break it along the score lines using a large knife.

Fancy Coconut Bonbons

MAKES 5 DOZEN; PICTURED ON PAGE 42

2 boxes (about 2 pounds) powdered sugar
1 can sweetened, condensed milk
1 teaspoon vanilla
2 pounds pecans, chopped

½ cup (1 stick) butter or margarine
2 7-ounce cans coconut
7 2-ounce squares semisweet chocolate
½ block paraffin wax (2 ounces)

YOU WILL ALSO NEED: DOUBLE BOILER, TOOTHPICKS FOR DIPPING, WAX PAPER

1. Combine sugar; sweetened, condensed milk; vanilla; pecans; butter; and coconut. Blend well, then chill the mixture.
2. Roll the dough into balls and refrigerate until hard.
3. In a double boiler, melt the chocolate and paraffin.
4. With toothpicks, dip the chilled balls into the chocolate mixture.
5. Place the bonbons on wax paper to dry and cool.

49

Sausage-Mushroom Caps
MAKES APPROXIMATELY 30 MUSHROOM CAPS

1½ pounds medium mushrooms (about 30)
½ pound pork sausage
½ cup mozzarella cheese, grated (optional)

½ cups seasoned breadcrumbs
Parsley for garnish

YOU WILL ALSO NEED: 10-INCH SKILLET, SLOTTED SPOON, PAPER TOWELS, 15½ X 10½-INCH JELLY ROLL PAN OR ROASTING PAN OR RIMMED COOKIE SHEET

1. Preheat the oven to 450°F.
2. Remove the stems from the mushrooms; chop the stems. Set aside.
3. In a skillet over medium heat, cook the sausage until well browned. With a slotted spoon, remove the sausage to paper towels to drain. Spoon off all but 2 tablespoons of the drippings from the skillet. (Add vegetable oil to the drippings, if needed, to equal 2 tablespoons.)
4. In hot drippings over medium heat, cook the mushroom stems until they're tender, about 10 minutes, stirring frequently. Remove the skillet from heat; stir in sausage, cheese, and breadcrumbs.
5. Fill mushroom caps with the sausage mixture. Place stuffed mushrooms in 15½ x 10½-inch jelly roll pan. Bake for 15 minutes.
6. Garnish with parsley.

Individualizing each place setting lets your guests know they're important. Here are some simple ways to say "We are glad you are here. This place was prepared especially for you."

- Gift-wrap chocolate truffles, each in its own tiny box. These can double as place cards if you add a nametag to each one.

- Personalize a Christmas ornament with your guest's name and the date of the party.

- Tie a festive ribbon through a Christmas cookie cutter and neatly tie the silverware to it.

- Place a personalized Christmas cookie on each plate instead of a place card.

- Place a unique holiday candle beside each place setting. If the candle is big enough, you may want to decorate it with the guest's name and party date.

- Accent your table with unusual napkin rings. (I recently found some tiny picture frames that are also napkin rings.)

- Place a tiny Christmas stocking beside each plate to hold the silverware, or tuck the napkin in it.

- Use the Christmas stocking as a place card. With a paint pen or glue and glitter, write the name of a guest on each.

I've come to trust the following entertaining ideas over the years. I hope these hints will help you as you exercise your gift of hospitality and make your guests feel welcome.

- A successful dinner party begins with good friends who enjoy being together or with people who enjoy meeting new acquaintances. Either combination makes for lively conversation.

- For a more formal meal, seat ladies and gentlemen alternately, trying not to seat couples together. Always consider personalities and interests when planning a seating arrangement.

- Have hors d'oeuvres ready when guests arrive.

- Stay near the door to greet guests as they arrive. This welcome sets the tone for the evening.

- Allow thirty minutes for guests to mingle before serving the meal.

- Hold the meal no longer than fifteen minutes for late arrivals.

- Keep your centerpiece low and unobtrusive so it doesn't interfere with conversation.

- Keep smiling! Accidents happen, but your guests' comfort is the top priority. Handle problems casually.

Eve

CHRISTMAS EVE

Knowing, but not telling. Keeping all of Santa's secrets tucked carefully away like hidden treasure. Parents whisper or spell out their secret plans. This one night of the year, children readily submit to bedtime, and visions of Santa flying overhead charm them to sleep. Mom and Dad finally crawl into bed in the wee hours of the morning, later than planned but with bicycles and dollhouses assembled, video camera ready, and a few bites of Santa's cookies and milk in their tummies. Christmas Eve...no matter how old you are, the excitement never goes away!

TO GRANDMOTHER'S HOUSE WE GO

In my treasure chest of memories, some of the most priceless gems are from Christmas Eve celebrations lovingly and forever etched on my heart. In my family, opening gifts on Christmas morning has always been a celebration shared with immediate family. But Christmas Eve is for extended family—Grandma and Grandpa, aunts and uncles, and lots and lots of cousins!

As I was growing up, we always spent Christmas Eve with my dad's relatives. He was from a large family, so there was lots of hustle and bustle at my grandparents' house. As a child, I found this exhilarating.

My grandmother was a wonderful hostess, not only to her family but also to the countless friends and strangers who made their way into her inviting kitchen. Her kitchen was rather small, but she made room around the table for everyone. As a matter of fact, there was always room for one more. Her creed, "the more the merrier," was adopted by the whole family and still stands today, a testament to her success in passing the baton of hospitality to her children and grandchildren.

A wonderful supper of everyone's favorite selections was served, and then our whole family would gather in the den. Gifts were always piled high around the Christmas tree, and usually my uncle W. T. (affectionately known as Uncle Dub) would "play Santa Claus" and hand them out. Paper would begin to fly, and shrieks of excitement were heard around the room. Many times I can remember standing amid what appeared to be a river of wrapping paper, waist deep. I loved to wade through it and hear it rustling under my feet, or fall into it much like I did the mound of leaves my dad had raked in autumn.

After the gifts had been opened, everyone pitched in to help my grandmother clean up the mess. Then we'd gather around the piano and sing every Christmas carol we knew—and improvise ones we didn't. There was something magical about opening our hearts and lifting our voices to the rafters together that brought such sweet harmony to our family. My grandfather would then stand and read from the Scriptures about the birth of Jesus, periodically removing his glasses to brush away tears as he shared with his family his greatest gift.

Christmas Eve is different now. In 1972 my parents moved us to Tennessee, where we've remained for the last thirty years. The focus of our Christmas Eve celebrations is now at my parents' home. They've become Grandma and Grandpa, and every Christmas Eve my brothers and I bring our own growing families to join them in keeping the old family tradition. We gather to enjoy a wonderful dinner crowded around my mom's table, and like the old days, there's always room for one more.

Then it's off to the den to exchange gifts and watch the children play with their toys, taking turns jumping in piles of discarded wrapping paper. Before long, my brother Trent moves to

the piano, where we gather and lift our voices in song together. Now it's my dad's turn to read from God's Word the story of our Savior's birth, and as he brushes away tears, I relish the wonderfully warm and familiar feeling. The tradition of being with family, of enjoying each other and loving God together, is one worth passing on. With each year, it is reborn richer and fuller than the year before.

"All thy children shall be taught of the LORD; and great shall be the peace of thy children."

Isaiah 54:13

CHRISTMAS DUST AND ASHES

It was Christmas Eve 1970, and my mother was scurrying around the kitchen making last-minute preparations before our family arrived for Christmas dinner. I was nine years old, excited about the upcoming festivities, and feeling in the holiday spirit—until my mother recruited me to do household chores. Trying to boost my suddenly flagging spirits, I decided to play my favorite Christmas albums on the stereo, light the Christmas tree, and burn candles to create an ambiance conducive to holiday dusting. Just as the music began and the candles were lit in the beautiful centerpiece that sat on my mother's grand piano, my grandmother called out to me: "Candy, I'm driving to the grocery store; would you like to come along?"

Here was my way of escape! Perhaps the relatives would have arrived by the time I got home, and it would be too late for dusting. I threw down my dustcloth and hurried out the door, gladly leaving everything behind.

Upon our return, my mother met me at the door, her face ashen and eyes moist with the residue of tears. "This Christmas was almost a very sad one," she said as she took me by the hand and led me to the family room. There I saw what had been our lovely grand piano, stand-

56

ing charred and smoldering. The candle I had left burning had ignited the surrounding greenery and set the instrument ablaze. The fire threatened more than our Christmas; it could have destroyed our home and our family. How quickly things we love can be gone!

Yet this disaster had a hidden blessing: It was the first time I had encountered such mercy. Not only had God mercifully protected my family, but my parents also extended to me unmerited favor. They saw how dreadful I felt about my mistake, and they never mentioned it again.

The concept of this wonderful gift—transgression deserving punishment but receiving a stay of execution—deeply impacted me again later in life, when I realized I was a sinner. Though I deserved death, I found life; when I should have received judgment, I received mercy. Jesus not only extended mercy—He took punishment in my place.

"Greater love hath no man than this, that a man lay down his life for his friends."

John 15:13

I Believe in Santa Claus

Do I believe in Santa Claus? Yes! Most certainly!
How do I know? Because I've seen him and sat upon his knee.
He has blue eyes that twinkle and hair that's turning gray,
And his belly shakes like jelly when he laughs at things I say.
He helps me with my prayers at night before he tucks me in,
Then kisses me on my face, and his whiskers tickle my chin.
At Christmastime he asks what I'd like written on his list
He works overtime on his job to see that nothing's missed.
I hear him tinkering in the garage, putting toys together.
My sister tried to catch a glimpse, but Santa wouldn't let her.
He's having so much fun, you see, he wants us to believe.
It would really disappoint him that I peeked on Christmas Eve.
That night he thought I was asleep, the house was lighted dimly;
I was trying to stay awake to see Santa slide down the chimney.
He didn't appear from the fireplace but descended the attic ladder.
I couldn't believe whose face I saw——then, my! What a clatter!
His arms piled high with gifts till he couldn't see the floor,
He crashed in the den, riding on my skateboard!
My sister's doll flew one way, a tricycle the other;
The Christmas tree would have toppled if it weren't for my mother!

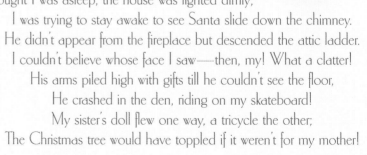

When the dust finally settled, he laughed, 'til tears rolled down his face;
Then by the light of a flickering candle, I saw Mom and Santa embrace!
Back to arranging gifts they went, and set my train 'round the tree;
When the job was done, they ate cookies from my sister and me.
That night I found the answer to a question asked through history:
"Who is this Santa Claus?" I have solved the mystery.
The one who travels from home to home all over the world,
Who makes a list and builds the toys for all good boys and girls
I have seen him, so I believe it, and it makes me kind of glad
To help him keep his secret—you see, Santa is my dad.

P.S. A couple of things I can't figure, that have baffled me all year:
Is my sister one of the elves? And where do we keep our deer?

CANDY CHRISTMAS

Christmas Turkey

PICTURED ON PAGE 60

1 fresh turkey (12 to 14 pounds), rinsed thoroughly and giblet packet removed

1½ bunches each fresh thyme, sage, basil, and oregano, coarsely chopped

1½ teaspoons each dried thyme, sage, basil, and oregano

2 tablespoons unsalted butter, softened

1 tablespoon salt

1 tablespoon freshly ground pepper

2 small onions, cut into ¼-inch slices

2 carrots, cut into ¼-inch rounds

2 stalks celery, cut into ¼-inch pieces

2 leeks, cut into ¼-inch rounds

2 cloves garlic, sliced

Olive oil

Herb Butter

1 cup (2 sticks) unsalted butter, softened

2 tablespoons each fresh parsley, sage, thyme, and basil, minced

1 tablespoon fresh oregano, minced

1 clove garlic, minced

Salt

Black pepper, freshly ground

YOU WILL ALSO NEED: STRING, ROASTING PAN AND RACK, MEAT THERMOMETER, SMALL BOWL

1. Preheat the oven to 450°F.
2. Mix together fresh herbs, dried herbs, 2 tablespoons butter, salt, and pepper. Rub into the turkey cavity.
3. Combine onions, carrots, celery, leeks, and garlic. Stuff into turkey cavity and truss the cavity with string.
4. Rub the outside of the bird with olive oil and place it on a rack in a roasting pan. Roast for 30 minutes.
5. Combine all ingredients for herb butter in a small bowl. (This can be refrigerated up to 4 days, but bring to room temperature before using.)
6. Reduce oven temperature to 325°F and brush the turkey with half of the Herb Butter. Roast another 30 minutes and brush with remaining herb butter. Continue to roast, basting occasionally with pan juices, until thigh temperature reaches 170°F on a meat thermometer (about 2 hours, 15 minutes).

Festive Field Greens

PICTURED ON PAGE 60

¾ pound mixed salad greens
Balsamic Vinaigrette (recipe
  follows)
4 ounces feta cheese
2 11-ounce cans Mandarin
  orange slices
1 pint strawberries, quartered
Sweet and Spicy Pecans (recipe
  follows)

Balsamic Vinaigrette
½ cup balsamic vinegar
3 tablespoons Dijon mustard
3 tablespoons honey
2 garlic cloves, minced
2 small shallots, minced
¼ teaspoon salt
¼ teaspoon pepper
1 cup olive oil

Sweet and Spicy Pecans
¼ cup plus 2 tablespoons sugar
1 cup warm water
1 cup pecan halves
1 tablespoon chili powder
⅛ teaspoon ground red pepper

YOU WILL ALSO NEED: 6 INDIVIDUAL PLATES; WIRE WHISK; COOKIE SHEET, LIGHTLY GREASED

1. Toss greens with balsamic vinaigrette and crumbled feta cheese. Place on 6 individual plates.
2. Arrange orange slices and strawberries over greens. Sprinkle top with sweet and spicy pecans.

Balsamic Vinaigrette

1. Whisk together all ingredients except olive oil.
2. Gradually whisk olive oil into the mixture.

Sweet and Spicy Pecans

1. Dissolve ¼ cup sugar in warm water. Add the pecan halves and soak for 10 minutes. Drain pecans, discarding the sugar mixture.
2. Combine 2 tablespoons sugar, chili powder, and red pepper. Add the pecans, tossing to coat. Place the pecans on a lightly greased cookie sheet. Bake at 350°F for 10 minutes or until pecans are golden brown, stirring once.

CANDY'S NOTE: The pecans can be prepared up to a week in advance; just place them in an airtight plastic bag and refrigerate. For even tastier results, add ¼ teaspoon of cayenne pepper or double the chili powder.

Sausage-Pecan Cornbread Dressing

MAKES 18 SERVINGS

2 cups cornmeal
½ cup all-purpose flour
2 teaspoons baking powder
1 teaspoon baking soda
1 teaspoon salt
1 teaspoon sugar (optional)
6 large eggs, divided
2 cups buttermilk

2 tablespoons butter or margarine
2 16-ounce packages ground pork sausage
½ cup (1 stick) butter or margarine
3 bunches green onions, chopped

4 celery stalks, chopped
1 16-ounce package herb-seasoned stuffing mix
3 32-ounce cans chicken broth
1 cup chopped pecans, toasted

YOU WILL ALSO NEED: LARGE BOWL, 10-INCH CAST-IRON SKILLET OR 9-INCH ROUND CAKE PAN, 9 X 13-INCH BAKING DISH OR 9-INCH SQUARE BAKING DISH

1. Preheat the oven to 425°F.
2. Combine cornmeal, flour, baking powder, baking soda, salt, and sugar (if desired) in a large bowl.
3. Stir together 2 eggs and buttermilk; add these to the dry ingredients, stirring just until moistened.
4. Melt 2 tablespoons butter in a skillet or cake pan by placing it in the oven. Stir into the batter. Pour the batter into the hot skillet.
5. Bake cornbread for 25 minutes or until golden; then cool and crumble.
6. If desired, freeze in a large, heavy-duty, air-tight plastic bag for up to 1 month. Thaw in the refrigerator.
7. Cook the sausage in a skillet over medium-high heat for 8 to 10 minutes, stirring until it crumbles and is no longer pink. Drain off the excess fat and wipe the skillet clean with a paper towel.
8. Melt ½ cup butter in the skillet over medium heat. Add green onions and celery, and sauté until tender.
9. In a large bowl, stir together the remaining 4 eggs; mix in cornbread, sausage, onion mixture, stuffing mix, chicken broth, and pecans. Spoon this into a lightly greased baking dish.
10. Reduce oven temperature to 350°F and bake for 1 hour or until browned.

Sweet Potato Casserole

MAKES 10 TO 12 SERVINGS; PICTURED ON PAGE 60

3 cups (about 4 medium to large) sweet
  potatoes
½ cup sugar
½ cup (1 stick) butter or margarine
2 eggs, beaten
1 teaspoon vanilla
⅓ cup milk

Topping

⅓ cup melted butter
1 cup light brown sugar
½ cup flour
1 cup chopped pecans

YOU WILL ALSO NEED: ELECTRIC MIXER, 9 X 13-INCH BAKING DISH

1. Preheat the oven to 350°F.
2. Peel and cut up potatoes. Boil for about 25 minutes, until tender. Drain well and mash.
3. Mix together potatoes, sugar, butter, eggs, vanilla, and milk. Spread in baking dish.

Topping

1. Mix ⅓ cup melted butter with the remaining topping ingredients. Sprinkle on the potato mixture.
2. Bake for 25 minutes.

Hazel Christmas's Light Rolls

PICTURED ON PAGE 60

1 cup buttermilk

½ cup shortening or butter

¼ cup honey

1 teaspoon salt

1 package yeast

¼ cup warm water

4 cups flour, divided

2 eggs, room temperature

YOU WILL ALSO NEED: SAUCEPAN; ELECTRIC MIXER;
9 X 12-INCH BAKING SHEET, GREASED

1. Heat buttermilk, shortening, honey, and salt just until shortening melts; cool slightly.
2. Dissolve the yeast in warm water.
3. When the milk mixture is lukewarm, mix with yeast, 2 cups flour, and eggs. Beat well. Add 1 cup of flour and beat well. Remove the beater and mix in ¾ cup flour by hand.
4. Grease the inside of a bowl to keep the dough from sticking. Cover the bowl with a dishtowel, and let the dough rise until it's double in size. Punch down. Use the remaining ¼ cup of flour for kneading. Make into rolls and let rise for about one hour.
5. Preheat the oven to 400°F. Bake rolls for 10 to 12 minutes.

CANDY'S NOTE: I use real butter instead of shortening. I've found that the less you knead these, the lighter they are. I usually use half white bread flour and half whole-wheat flour because my family prefers whole-wheat rolls.

This recipe has been in my husband's family for many years and was given to me by my dear mother-in-law, Hazel Christmas. She is a master at the craft of bread making and has been instrumental in honing my bread-making skills.

Holiday Nut Tart

MAKES 8 TO 10 SERVINGS

Tart Shell

⅓ cup butter or margarine

¼ cup granulated sugar

1 egg yolk

1 cup all-purpose flour

Filling

1 cup coarsely chopped walnuts

1 cup coarsely chopped pecans
(or you can use 2 cups of any
kind of nut)

¼ cup butter or margarine

⅔ cup light brown sugar,
packed

¼ cup dark corn syrup

½ cup heavy cream, divided

YOU WILL ALSO NEED: WOODEN SPOON OR ELECTRIC MIXER, MEDIUM BOWL, 9-INCH FLUTED TART PAN WITH OR WITHOUT REMOVABLE BOTTOM, WIRE RACK, BAKING SHEET, HEAVY 2-QUART SAUCEPAN

Tart Shell

1. Preheat the oven to 375°F.
2. In a medium-sized bowl, with wooden spoon or electric mixer, beat butter and granulated sugar until light and fluffy. Add the egg yolk and beat well. Gradually beat in flour, just until blended. (Mixture will be crumbly.)
3. Form the dough into a ball and press into the bottom and side of the tart pan. Bake on the center rack of the oven for 12 minutes or until lightly browned. Cool completely on a wire rack.

Filling

1. Spread nuts on a baking sheet in a single layer. Bake at 375°F for 4 minutes, then set aside to cool.
2. Sprinkle the nuts in the bottom of the tart shell.
3. In the saucepan, melt butter and stir in light brown sugar, corn syrup, and 2 tablespoons of heavy cream. Bring to a boil over medium heat, stirring constantly; boil for 1 minute.
4. Pour the sugar mixture over the nuts. Bake at 375°F on the center rack of the oven for 10 minutes, just until mixture is bubbly. Cool on wire rack.
5. Beat the remaining cream just until stiff. Refrigerate until serving time.
6. Serve the tart at room temperature with a bowl of chilled whipped cream.

CANDY'S NOTE: You can use just one type of nut in this recipe, but the combination of walnuts and pecans is very tasty and makes for a nice presentation.

66

Pumpkin Crunch Torte

PICTURED ON PAGE 37

1 15-ounce can pumpkin pie mix
1 15-ounce can evaporated milk
1 cup sugar
3 eggs
1 package yellow cake mix
½ cup chopped pecans

1 cup (2 sticks) butter or margarine, melted
1 8-ounce package cream cheese, softened
1 cup whipped topping, room temperature
1 cup powdered sugar
1 teaspoon vanilla
Toasted pecans for garnish (optional)

YOU WILL ALSO NEED: ELECTRIC MIXER, 10-INCH SPRINGFORM PAN, PARCHMENT OR WAX PAPER, FLAT SERVING PLATTER, BAKING SHEET

1. Preheat the oven to 350°F.
2. Mix together pumpkin pie mix, evaporated milk, sugar, and eggs until well blended.
3. Line the pan with parchment paper or wax paper. Pour in the pumpkin mixture and carefully sprinkle dry cake mix evenly across the top. Sprinkle nuts over the cake mix. Pour melted butter over all.
4. Bake for 50 to 60 minutes or until the top is lightly browned. Let cool completely, then remove the springform ring and invert the torte onto a flat serving platter.
5. Mix together cream cheese, whipped topping, powdered sugar, and vanilla. Spread on top of the pumpkin layer.
6. Refrigerate until ready to serve.
7. Garnish with toasted pecans, if desired. Toast pecans in an oven preheated to 350°F. Spread pecans in a single layer on an ungreased baking sheet. Bake 10 to 15 minutes, stirring occasionally, until pecans are golden brown. Cool completely before adding to torte.

Cookies & Cream Cheesecake

PICTURED ON PAGE 60

Crust

3 cups Oreo cookie crumbs
9 tablespoons butter or
   margarine, melted
1 cup sugar

Filling

4 8-ounce packages cream
   cheese, softened
1½ cups sugar
6 large eggs

1 teaspoon vanilla
1½ cups Oreo cookies,
   broken into large pieces

YOU WILL ALSO NEED: 9-INCH SPRINGFORM PAN, GREASED; ELECTRIC MIXER; FOOD PROCESSOR (OPTIONAL); ALUMINUM FOIL (OPTIONAL)

Crust

1. Combine cookie crumbs, butter, and 1 cup sugar. Mix well.
2. Press the mixture into the bottom and 2 inches up sides of the pan. Chill.

Filling

1. Preheat the oven to 300°F.
2. Combine cream cheese and 1½ cups sugar; beat until smooth and fluffy. Add eggs, one at a time, beating well after each addition. Mix in the vanilla, then carefully fold in the cookie pieces.
3. Pour the batter into the prepared crust. Bake for 90 minutes.
4. Turn the oven off, open the door slightly, and let the cheesecake cool in the oven for an additional hour. Remove cheesecake from the pan. Chill before serving.

CANDY'S NOTE: For the best cookie crumbs, I use a food processor to grind the Oreos into crumb form. Also, the secret to baking a perfect cheesecake, with no cracks in the center, is to wrap the bottom and sides of the springform pan tightly with 2 or 3 layers of aluminum foil until it is leak-proof. Pour 1 inch of water into a larger baking pan and set springform pan in the water. Bake as directed. (Cracks in cheesecake result from a lack of moisture. As the water in the pan evaporates, it adds moisture to the atmosphere inside the oven.)

- Give each guest a candle. Light your candle from one in the center of the room. Share what you feel is the true meaning of Christmas, then light the candle of the next person. Have each guest share in this way for a special conclusion to the evening's activities.

- Potluck meals work great for Christmas Eve. The responsibility is shared, and everyone's favorite recipe is featured.

- Adopt a family in need and surprise them on Christmas Eve with goodies for all.

- Visit the bookstore or library and bring home a new Christmas book to read to your younger guests.

- Ask each guest ahead of time to prepare a poem, song, or skit to share on Christmas Eve. This takes some of the focus away from gifts and puts it on the special people in your life.

- Modern technology is great! If your children are grown, find your favorite Christmas photos of them. Scan the old photos and enlarge them, then frame them and place them throughout your home. They'll bring back great memories, and your grandkids will love seeing their parents as kids themselves.

- When guests arrive for your party, give each person three candy canes. Explain that every time someone hears them say, "me," they have to give the other person a candy cane. At the end of the evening, the person with the most candy canes wins a prize.

HOLLY BERRY CENTERPIECE

You will need:

Newspaper (or something to protect work surface)
Gold spray paint (or color of your choice)
1 6-inch Styrofoam craft cone
1 garland of holly berries
   (from a craft store)
Gold and red glitter
Ribbon
Wire cutters or garden shears
Bow, poinsettias, and
other decorations

1. On a well-covered surface, spray-paint Styrofoam cone; allow to dry.

2. With wire cutters or garden shears, clip berry bunches from garland, keeping stems with berries (to attach to cone).

3. Starting at the bottom of the cone, press each bunch firmly into cone, going around to form the first row. Then move up cone to form the next row, and so on until cone is completely covered.

4. On a well-covered surface, spray tree with remaining paint. While the paint is still wet, sprinkle with gold glitter. Allow to dry, about 3 hours.

5. Dot a few berries with glue and sprinkle with red glitter, giving illusion of ornaments. Decorate top with bow, poinsettias, etc.

CANDY'S NOTE: This is also pretty with berries left red instead of painted gold.

Christmas

CHAPTER Five

CHRISTMAS MORNING

Few things in life are more fun than watching a child enter the room on Christmas morning. Videotapes roll and cameras flash as youngsters squeal with delight when they open just the right gift. Children dig to the bottom of stockings overflowing with trinkets and candy. Parents vicariously relive the fun of a new bike, the joy of a new baby doll, or the excitement of a remote-control car. It's Christmas morning, when all adults wish, just for a season, that they were still children.

Morning

WORTH THE WAIT

Christmas morning in our home is thrilling…and chaotic! It's the moment my children have waited for since the first sign of blustery weather. It's finally time to open the gifts they've examined, weighed, and shaken. If I had a dime for every time I've heard "Just one more hint, Mom…please!" I could have a free trip to Bermuda for the New Year!

My children are night owls. Even though their regular bedtime is 8:30, they take full advantage of every opportunity to stay up late at night and sleep late the next morning—or as they say, "until the cows come home." Every week they count down the days until Saturday morning, when they're allowed to sleep as long as they want. But not on Christmas morning. On that day, Nicholas and Jasmine fly out of their beds at the first light of sunrise and descend, along with both of our dogs, on my husband and me. Squealing and laughing, they jump onto our bed; the excitement causes the dogs to bark, adding the finishing touch to utter chaos.

Generally, I'm incoherent until I've had my first cup of coffee. On this morning, however, I'm awakened with such a start that more times than not, the coffee has to wait. But I don't mind.

I believe the anticipation of a coming Christmas is almost as much fun as Christmas itself. It builds to such a tenor that children can hardly bear it, thus heightening their enthusiasm on Christmas morning.

I learned this at the age of six, when my dad's younger sister Brenda gave me a beautifully wrapped mystery gift. She had delivered the gift to our home early in the season, so it sat under our tree almost from the moment it was trimmed. One day, I was examining the gift (as I did every day) and noticed in the wrapping paper a tiny rip the size of a pinhole. I remember lying under the tree day after day, peering through the hole, trying with all my might to discern what was inside. For days I was unsuccessful, but the tiny tear grew "mysteriously" larger over time. Finally, the mystery of the package was revealed: It held a Barbie canopy bed with a lace comforter and accessories. It was beautiful…for a moment. Then disappointment settled over me like a dark cloud. The excitement was over, and the lure of the forbidden was gone—because I knew.

Christmas isn't confined to one morning of opening gifts; it's the whole package surrounding that event. It's the hoping, wishing, and waiting. It's the imagination that wants to believe in Santa Claus even though you know he doesn't exist. It's the feeling that starts in your tummy and rises until it jumps out of your mouth in a giggle or that causes you to skip instead of walk. It's the thrill that makes kids want to kiss Mom or Dad and squeeze them until they're afraid they might break.

Throughout the Christmas season, Kent and I channel much of our energy into reaching out

to friends and business associates, connecting with relatives through the cards and gifts we mail. On Christmas morning, however, our focus is on our little family and watching our children's dreams come true.

"If ye then…know how to give good gifts unto your children, how much more shall your Father which is in heaven give good things to them that ask him?"

Matthew 7:11

TRADITIONS

GRANDFATHER'S GIFT

My grandfather was one of the most wonderful men I've ever known. He was a minister of the gospel, answering the call of God on his life when he was just twenty years old. He spent most of his life pioneering churches across the country before serving for forty years as the pastor of one congregation in Louisiana. He was a man of prayer and a faithful soldier of the cross. I revered my grandfather for his inner strength but cherished him for his keen sensitivity to the needs of his family and his flock, both of whom he loved dearly.

Born in 1893, Reverend W. T. Hemphill had lived a full, active life of sixty-eight years before I was born. By the time I reached adolescence, my grandfather's physical strength had waned considerably. A horrendous fall had crushed his hip and leg, rendering him immobile and temporarily confining him to a wheelchair. My family faced the grim reality that my grandfather would not live forever. We found it nearly impossible to conceive of a world without him. But instead of allowing a dark cloud of dread and gloom to hover over us, we collectively decided, without ever verbalizing it, that we would savor each Christmas as if it would be his last. No melancholy, no sadness—just living each moment to its fullest. We lived by an unwritten creed: The differences every family invariably experiences were to be set aside. We would feast more heartily, fellowship longer, and laugh deeper. We'd sing with more passion, hug each other tighter, and let no "I love you" be left unsaid. What wonderful times we shared!

The Lord was merciful to us. He extended my grandfather's life several years beyond the doctor's original projection. One of the many blessings his prolonged life afforded us was the time for our family's practice to become habit. The traditions born of our love for him continue now, long after his death. Our family gatherings and relationships are heartier, deeper, more passionate, and stronger. We still say "I love you" every chance we get.

I used to think my grandfather's life was the adhesive that held our family together. Now I recognize that although we'll always love him deeply and cherish our memories of him, it was more than my grandfather's life that drew our family together. It was the example of Christ in him. That example now lives on in my remaining family. We've learned that as long as Christ is the focus of our Christmas holiday and the center of our joy, no loss or heartbreak can ever separate us from each other or from the love of God.

"I am persuaded, that neither death, nor life, nor angels, nor principalities, nor powers, nor things present, nor things to come, nor height, nor depth, nor any other creature, shall be able to separate us from the love of God, which is in Christ Jesus our Lord."

Romans 8:38–39

Christmas in Heaven

I found an old picture book from Christmases yesteryear,
I looked on faces that long have gone, and brushed away a tear.
"If I could just go back," I said, "but my children weren't yet born."
I stood between the past and present and felt a little torn.
I longed to be with those who've passed yet remain with loved ones now;
My joy would be complete to make them one, somehow.
Then a thought struck me, the answer I'd like to find,
"Will there be Christmas in heaven?" resounded in my mind.
"Why not?" I said. "We'll see Jesus in that place;
We can celebrate His birth with Him face to face."
Then our family from every generation could share Christmas together.
My grandpa will hold my son on his knee and talk with him forever.
My grandmother's face will glow with youth; she'll stand straight and strong.
Arm in arm, she'll lead us all in a yuletide song.
I was suddenly so excited, my tears turned to laughter.
No more wishing for what was, just the happy ever after.
That night I couldn't fall asleep till half past eleven
Because I have decided there will be Christmas in heaven.

CANDY CHRISTMAS

Cranberry-Orange Scones

2 cups all-purpose flour
10 teaspoons granulated sugar, divided
1 tablespoon grated orange peel
2 teaspoons baking powder
½ teaspoon salt
¼ teaspoon baking soda
⅓ cup butter or margarine, cold
1 cup dried cranberries

¼ cup orange juice
¼ cup half-and-half
1 egg
1 tablespoon milk

Glaze (optional)

½ cup powdered sugar
1 tablespoon orange juice

YOU WILL ALSO NEED: MEDIUM BOWL, SMALL BOWL, BAKING SHEET

1. Preheat the oven to 400°F.
2. Combine flour, 7 teaspoons of granulated sugar, orange peel, baking powder, salt, and baking soda. Cut in butter until the mixture resembles coarse crumbs; set aside.
3. In a small bowl, combine cranberries, orange juice, half-and-half, and egg.
4. Add the cranberry mixture to the flour mixture and stir until a soft dough forms.
5. On a floured surface, gently knead the dough 6 to 8 times. Pat the dough into an 8-inch circle. Cut the dough into 10 wedges. Separate the wedges and place them on an ungreased baking sheet.
6. Brush the wedges with milk and sprinkle with remaining sugar. Bake for 12 to 15 minutes or until lightly browned.

Glaze

1. If desired, combine glaze ingredients.
2. Drizzle over scones. Serve warm.

Sausage and Egg Casserole

8 eggs

1½ tablespoons dry mustard

3 cups milk

Salt

Pepper

2½ pounds sausage

8 or 9 slices of white bread, cubed

10 ounces sharp cheddar cheese, grated

YOU WILL ALSO NEED: 9 X 12-INCH CASSEROLE DISH, COOKING SPRAY

1. Coat the inside of a casserole dish with cooking spray.
2. Beat together eggs, dry mustard, milk, and salt and pepper to taste.
3. Brown the sausage and drain well.
4. Layer bread, sausage, and cheese; repeat. Pour the egg mixture over the top and refrigerate overnight.
5. Bake for 1 hour in a preheated 350°F oven.

Chicken Brunch Bake

3 cups chicken broth

1 10¾-ounce can condensed cream of chicken soup

9 slices day-old bread, cubed

4 cups cooked chicken or ham, cubed

½ cup uncooked instant rice

1 cup sharp cheddar cheese, grated and divided

2 tablespoons fresh parsley, minced

1½ teaspoons salt

4 eggs, beaten

YOU WILL ALSO NEED: 9 X 13-INCH BAKING DISH, GREASED; LARGE BOWL

1. Preheat the oven to 325°F. Grease baking dish.
2. In a large bowl, blend together broth and cream of chicken soup. Add the bread cubes and toss to coat. Add chicken or ham, rice, ¾ cup cheese, parsley, and salt; mix well.
3. Transfer this mixture to the baking dish. Pour eggs over all and sprinkle with remaining cheese.
4. Bake, uncovered, for 1 hour or until a knife inserted near the center comes out clean.

Hash-Brown Casserole

2 10¾-ounce cans condensed cream of potato soup
1 8-ounce carton sour cream
½ teaspoon garlic salt
1 2-pound package frozen hash-brown potatoes
2 cups (8 ounces) cheddar cheese, grated
½ cup Parmesan cheese, grated

YOU WILL ALSO NEED: 9 X 13-INCH BAKING DISH, GREASED; LARGE BOWL

1. Preheat the oven to 350°F.
2. In a large bowl, combine the soup, sour cream, and garlic salt. Add hash-brown potatoes and cheddar cheese; mix well.
3. Pour the mixture into the baking dish and top with Parmesan cheese. Bake, uncovered, for 55 to 60 minutes or until potatoes are tender.

Southern-Gal Biscuits

MAKES 18 BISCUITS

2 cups flour
2 teaspoons baking powder
½ teaspoon cream of tartar
½ teaspoon salt
2 tablespoons sugar
½ cup shortening
⅔ cup buttermilk
1 egg

YOU WILL ALSO NEED: BISCUIT CUTTER; ROLLING PIN; BAKING PAN OR IRON SKILLET, GREASED

1. Preheat the oven to 450°F.
2. Sift together the dry ingredients. Blend in shortening, buttermilk, and egg. Knead for 5 minutes.
3. On floured surface, roll out dough to ½-inch thickness.
4. With biscuit cutter, cut the dough and place biscuits in pan or skillet. Bake for 10 to 15 minutes.

Cheesy Grits Casserole

MAKES 6 TO 8 SERVINGS; PICTURED ON PAGE 78

4 cups water
1 teaspoon salt
1 cup quick-cooking grits
2 cups (8 ounces) sharp cheddar cheese, grated

⅔ cup milk
⅓ cup butter or margarine
1 teaspoon Worcestershire sauce
4 large eggs, lightly beaten
Paprika

YOU WILL ALSO NEED: LARGE SAUCEPAN; 2-QUART CASSEROLE DISH, GREASED

1. Preheat the oven to 350°F.
2. In a large saucepan, bring to boil water and salt.
3. Stir in the grits. Return to a boil.
4. Cover, reduce heat, and simmer for 5 minutes, stirring occasionally.
5. Remove the saucepan from heat. Add cheese, milk, butter, and Worcestershire sauce, stirring until the cheese and butter melt. Add the eggs and stir well.
6. Spoon this mixture into the casserole dish and sprinkle with paprika.
7. Bake, uncovered, for 1 hour or until thoroughly heated and lightly browned. Let stand for 5 minutes before serving.

82

Sticky Buns

MAKES 18 BUNS

1 recipe of Hazel Christmas's Light Rolls dough (page 65)

1¼ cups dark brown sugar, firmly packed

5 tablespoons butter or margarine

½ cup water

1 cup pecans, chopped and divided

3 tablespoons granulated sugar

2 teaspoons ground cinnamon

YOU WILL ALSO NEED: ROLLING PIN, HEAVY SAUCEPAN, JUMBO MUFFIN PANS (FOR 18 BUNS), WAX PAPER, WIRE RACK

1. Punch down the Light Rolls dough and transfer it to a floured surface. Roll out to an 18 x 12-inch rectangle.
2. Combine brown sugar, butter, and water in heavy saucepan. Bring to a gentle boil and cook for 10 minutes, until thick and syrupy. Place 1 tablespoon of mixture in the bottom of each muffin cup. Sprinkle with ½ cup pecans.
3. Combine granulated sugar, cinnamon, and remaining pecans. Sprinkle over the dough in an even layer. Roll up tightly, from the long side, to form a cylinder.
4. Cut the cylinder into 1-inch rounds and place in muffin pan. Leave to rise in a warm place until increased by half, about 30 minutes.
5. Preheat the oven to 350°F. Bake until golden, about 25 minutes. Remove from the oven and invert the pan onto a sheet of wax paper. Leave for 3 to 5 minutes, then lift the pan from the buns. Transfer buns to a wire rack to cool. Serve sticky-side up.

Lemon-Cranberry Mini Loaves
MAKES 8 TO 10 MINI LOAVES; PICTURED ON PAGE 78

⅔ cup butter or margarine, softened
1½ cups sugar
3 tablespoons lemon juice
2 tablespoons grated lemon peel
4 eggs
3 cups all-purpose flour
2 teaspoons baking powder
2 teaspoons salt

1 cup milk
2 cups dried cranberries
1 cup chopped walnuts

Glaze

¼ cup sugar
¼ cup lemon juice

YOU WILL ALSO NEED: 8-TO-10 5 X 3 X 2-INCH MINI LOAF PANS, GREASED; ELECTRIC MIXER; TOOTHPICK OR SKEWER; WIRE RACKS

1. Preheat the oven to 350°F.
2. In a mixing bowl, cream together butter, sugar, lemon juice, and lemon peel. Add the eggs, one at a time, beating well after each addition.
3. In a separate bowl, combine flour, baking powder, and salt; add to the creamed mixture alternately with milk. Stir in cranberries and walnuts.
4. Pour batter into loaf pans and bake for 40 to 45 minutes or until a toothpick inserted near the center comes out clean. Cool for 10 minutes before removing from pans to wire racks.
5. With a toothpick or skewer, poke 12 holes in each loaf.

Glaze

1. Combine sugar and lemon juice until sugar is dissolved.
2. Spoon over loaves. Cool completely before slicing.

LAGNIAPPE

At our house we eat Christmas breakfast on fine china and crystal, but we wear our Christmas pajamas. However you share Christmas morning, be sure to enjoy each other and have fun! Here are some other hints:

- Prepare breakfast casseroles ahead of time, and choose quick and easy recipes for everything else.

- Serve breakfast coffee cake or sweet rolls in the living room. Everyone can eat and open gifts at the same time.

- Let your children give their gifts to parents and siblings first as a way to focus on giving more than receiving. They'll feel pride, a sense of accomplishment, and the joy of giving.

- After the gifts have been opened, show a video from some past Christmases.

- If grandparents aren't present as kids open gifts, be sure to take pictures or videotape the event to share with them later.

- Leave cookies and a card for your mail carrier and your newspaper delivery person. They deserve your thanks, and they will appreciate your thinking of them.

- Make sure one of your gifts to your family is something the whole family can do together.

- As soon as you wake up, put on the Christmas music.

- A colorful Christmas quilt makes a great tablecloth, or use it on the ground for a morning picnic.

- Sugared fruit makes a festive treat for Christmas morning. Just dip the fruit in egg white and then roll it in sugar.

- Stocking stuffers are often the best part of the morning. Jump ropes, stickers, cars, crayons, and yo-yos are great for little ones. Think about gift certificates, bubble bath, golf balls, and jewelry for your older kids.

- Choose a theme and plan a progressive supper in your neighborhood. Everyone gets to see more houses decorated while sharing the time and expense of the menu.

- If you have a guitar or a piano, sit around the room and sing all your families favorite carols. If you don't have instruments, turn on the radio and listen to the top 40 Christmas countdown.

- Buy a new Christmas book each year. Read it to your children, even if they think they're too old. They'll appreciate it later!

- Each year buy a family tree ornament—something that reminds you of the past year. If you can't find one to buy, make one using pictures you have taken.

Day

CHRISTMAS DAY

It's Christmas Day! The smell of turkey or ham permeates the house. Early this morning, ribbons, bows, and brightly colored packages filled the room. Now the gifts have been opened, and large garbage bags filled with the remnants of a month's shopping line the hallway, waiting for Dad to do his job. Hugs and genuine thank-yous have been sufficiently passed around, and children are strangely quiet as they read a new book or race a new car. It's time to relax and enjoy the gifts—but not just the ones purchased with money. The real treasures of this day are the ones money can't buy: spending a day off with a child, putting together a puzzle with cousins from another state, or throwing a football with Grandpa. Christmas Day is full of such hidden treasures. Look for them all day long, and enjoy your gifts!

PAGEANTS, PRESENTS, AND PRICE TAGS

Every year it was the same at our little church's Christmas pageant: "C is for the Christ child," we were reminded by a parade of little children who crossed the platform but never could seem to remember their lines. Year after year a new crop of bathrobe-clad shepherds faithfully proclaimed, "Let us go to Bethlehem and see this thing which is come to pass," their heads draped in bath towels. It never was the slick, professional production some churches had. But we loved our simple pageant more than we would have any expensive production. We never tired of it. To be perfectly honest, I still haven't tired of it. My family's lives were deeply rooted in our faith and our little church. Most of our social events and activities revolved around our little congregation. We looked forward to that humble Christmas pageant all year long.

Other happy childhood memories also revolve around faith and family. The emphasis in our home wasn't on material possessions, but rather on the birth of the Christ child, Jesus, and on moments shared with family and friends. I was not raised in great wealth.

My parents couldn't afford to lavish my brothers and me with gifts, but we never felt deprived. On the contrary, we were content and secure in the love our parents lavished on us. It is this gift, not any expensive presents I may have received, that stands out so clearly in my mind.

In today's society, it's common to know the price of everything, but the value of little. It is my hope that I can teach my children—and remind myself—that it isn't the gift we hold in our hands, but the gift of Jesus in our hearts that makes us rich.

"In whom we have redemption through his blood,
the forgiveness of sins,
according to the riches of his grace."

Ephesians 1:7

In October of 1993, my husband, Kent, our five-year-old daughter Jasmine, and I took a trip to Concord, California. We planned to stay for two weeks, as my husband and I both had scheduled busy speaking tours in the area. We decided to seize this opportunity to visit dear friends who lived nearby.

We were excited about our trip, but when we arrived, I wasn't feeling well. I was six months pregnant, and it became apparent that I wouldn't be able to do all the things we'd planned. Growing up singing gospel music and traveling on a bus with my family had taught me that complaining doesn't help anything and that the show must go on. So I quietly went about my duties as wife, mother, and minister—miserable the whole time. But then I started having pains that grew to be unbearable.

I called my doctor in Nashville and described my symptoms. With the information that I provided, he suggested that I was suffering from muscle spasms. He recommended a hot bath and a few exercises and said the symptoms should soon subside. I was awake all that night, trying to find a way to ease the pain. But by morning it had worsened, and I had begun to hemorrhage.

HOME FOR CHRISTMAS

My friend Marilyn, with whom I was staying at the time, called a doctor friend of hers and asked him to come by and help me with my muscle spasms. When the doctor arrived and saw the state I was in, he said, "I don't need to treat her for muscle spasms; I need to get her to the hospital as quickly as possible. She's in labor!"

With his wife and my husband in tow, the doctor rushed me to Mount Diablo Medical Center. The trip was like a scene out of a movie as he darted between cars, raced along the shoulder, and wove through crowded streets. He just shook his head as angry drivers called him all sorts of names. If I ever doubted that I had guardian angels, I became convinced that day that I do. Surely they were working overtime—and may have asked for a transfer when the drive was over!

We arrived safely and just in time for Nicholas Kent Christmas to be born. He weighed only two pounds. His birth set us on an unexpected long journey as we waited for our son to grow stronger. It would take all the pages in this book and many more its size to recount all the miracles the Lord preformed on Nicholas's behalf.

Our son was in intensive care for about three months. We were 2,500 miles from home, but wild horses couldn't have dragged us away from his bedside. Still, my heart was torn because Jasmine was too young to enter the ICU to visit except on certain days. She spent most of her time in the waiting room with either her dad or me as we took turns visiting the baby. Jasmine was such a trooper; she never complained.

As Christmastime approached and Nicholas gained strength, I felt a sense of debt to Jasmine. We had moved her from one house to the next as we stayed with various friends. Most nights, she slept on the floor. I'm sure she had feelings of uncertainty, just as we did, during our time of crisis. I longed to regain a sense of normalcy for Jasmine for the

holiday and had a growing desire to give her a wonderful Christmas with our family in Tennessee. This meant we would have to leave Nicholas in the care of his primary nurses for the three days we would be away.

We had kept a vigil at Nicholas's crib for weeks, overseeing his medical care and praying him through every physical difficulty. To relinquish those reins of control was almost more than I could bear. Fear seized my mind, and I imagined every worst-case scenario that could occur while I was away. I felt as though I were drowning and couldn't draw my next breath. But I knew this was something I needed to do for Jasmine.

The arrangements were made, and we arrived in Nashville the day before Christmas Eve. I believe this was the best Christmas Jasmine had ever experienced up to that point in her young life. We hadn't seen our family much during our ordeal, so the gathering was like a family reunion. This also had a healing effect on Kent and me that I had not anticipated. Our family was acutely aware of how emotionally exhausted we were, so they lavished on us an abundance of love.

Our time together was sweet, but I couldn't keep my heart and mind from wandering to the crib of a little black-haired, brown-eyed baby boy so many miles from me. My arms ached to hold him.

On Christmas morning Kent and I boarded a plane back to California for what we'd been told would be another two- or three-week stay. The airplane couldn't fly fast enough to suit me. Kent and I were so anxious and excited to see our son, to touch him and hold him close and smell his soft skin. We arrived in San Francisco late in the evening, rented a car, and raced to get to Oakland Children's Hospital before visiting hours ended. We rushed inside, impatiently rode the elevator, then scurried down the long hall to his nursery crib. Kent and I just stood there and wept at the sight of our son, sleeping so peacefully.

What happened then, some may call luck, fate, or coincidence. I call it the hand of God. We had arrived just as Dr. David Foster was making his last evening rounds. He quietly watched our reunion and, with charts in hand, calmly asked, "Would you like to take him home?"

"Oh yeah, sure," we replied, thinking he was joking.

Dr. Foster asked, more seriously this time, "Would you like to take him home?"

We could hardly believe our ears! Our emotions soared—we were laughing and crying as Dr. Foster said, "Nicholas Christmas is going home on Christmas. How do you like that?"

Excitedly, we packed all of his little belongings—his clothes, blankets, and toys. We said an emotional good-bye to the nurses, who had become our second family for the last three months, then bundled up our little Christmas miracle and took him home. What a wonderful gift!

Only one Christmas gift could ever be more precious to me than taking home our healthy baby boy. Another baby was the first and best Christmas gift: Jesus, God's Son, the true reason for celebrating this season.

"For unto us a child is born, unto us a son is given:... and his name shall be called Wonderful, Counsellor, The mighty God, The everlasting Father, The Prince of Peace."

Isaiah 9:6

Mary Held the Little Lamb

Mary held the little lamb
Closely to her breast,
And sang to Him a lullaby
With love and tenderness.
While shepherds watched and glory streamed
From heaven up above,
She smiled at those who brought their gifts
And held God's gift of love.
Mary held the little Lamb
While angels sang above
Of joy and cheer and tidings glad,
Of peace on earth and love.
She looked upon His face aglow
And thought of grace divine
And cradled in her arms so dear
The hope of all mankind.
Mary held the little Lamb
Born on Christmas day
'Neath heaven's brightest shining star
And placed Him on the hay—
Jesus Christ, the Lamb of God
She placed Him on the hay.

Words and music: Joel and LaBreeska Hemphill

Toasted-Walnut Salad

Walnut Dressing

⅔ cup walnut oil
⅓ cup fresh lemon juice
½ teaspoon Dijon mustard
¾ teaspoon sugar
Dash salt
Dash freshly ground pepper

Toasted Walnuts

1 large egg white
1 tablespoon water
1 cup brown sugar, packed
1½ cups walnuts

Salad

4 heads Boston lettuce, torn
2 ounces (½ cup) blue cheese, crumbled
1 apple; peeled, cored, and thinly sliced

YOU WILL ALSO NEED: JAR WITH LID, BAKING SHEET, SALAD BOWL

Walnut Dressing

1. Combine walnut oil, lemon juice, mustard, sugar, salt, and pepper in a covered jar.
2. Shake well and refrigerate.

Toasted Walnuts

1. Preheat the oven to 300°F.
2. Using fork, beat egg white and water in medium bowl until foamy. Add brown sugar and stir until the sugar dissolves. Add walnuts and toss to coat. Spread walnuts in a single layer on an ungreased baking sheet.
3. Bake 5 to 10 minutes, stirring occasionally, until walnuts are toasted.

Salad

1. In a salad bowl, toss together lettuce, toasted walnuts, blue cheese, and apple.
2. Add dressing, toss, and serve immediately.

Beef Wellington

MAKES 8 SERVINGS; PICTURED ON PAGE 96

1 pound medium mushrooms, divided

1 medium onion, minced

¼ cup butter or margarine

½ teaspoon black pepper (optional)

¼ teaspoon thyme leaves

1½ teaspoons salt

2 boxes Pepperidge Farms Puff Pastry

1 4-pound beef ribeye roast

2 eggs, separated

4 teaspoons water, divided

Curly endive for garnish

YOU WILL ALSO NEED: SKILLET, PAPER TOWELS, ROLLING PIN, SMALL BOWL, PASTRY BRUSH, BAKING SHEET, PANCAKE TURNER, WARM PLATTER

1. Preheat oven to 400°F.
2. Remove the stems from 10 mushrooms and set aside.
3. Mince the onion and the remaining mushrooms, including stems.
4. In skillet, melt butter and sauté minced mushrooms and onion until liquid evaporates (5 minutes).
5. Sprinkle mushroom mixture with pepper, thyme, and salt; allow this mixture to cool.
6. Prepare the pastry according to package directions. You may need to thaw the pastry for 30 to 40 minutes, until pliable. Divide the pastry into 5 equal pieces.
7. Trim fat from the roast and cut the meat in half lengthwise. Slice each half crosswise into 5 equal pieces. Dry the pieces of meat with paper towels.
8. On a floured surface, roll pastry to a 14 x 11-inch rectangle; cut in half to make two smaller pieces and trim edges to make neat rectangles. Reserve scraps.
9. Place ⅓ cup mushroom mixture in the center of each pastry rectangle. Top each with a piece of meat, sprinkled lightly with salt, and 1 sliced mushroom.
10. In a small bowl, beat egg whites and 2 teaspoons water with a fork; brush the mixture over the pastry edges. Fold the pastry over the meat and mushroom, overlapping the edges, and press to seal. Place on a baking sheet. Refrigerate while preparing remainder of dish.
11. Roll out remaining pastry scraps and, with a sharp knife, cut into a shape of your choice. Brush the backs with egg white and arrange them on top of the Wellingtons.
12. In a cup, beat egg yolks with 2 teaspoons water; brush this mixture over pastry.
13. Bake on cookie sheet 25 minutes for rare, 27 minutes for medium doneness. With pancake turner, place Wellingtons on warm platter. Garnish with curly endive, if desired. Serve immediately.

Parmesan Roasted Potatoes

½ cup Parmesan cheese, finely grated

½ cup all-purpose flour

1 teaspoon salt

¼ teaspoon black pepper

3½ pounds red potatoes, peeled and quartered lengthwise

½ cup (1 stick) unsalted butter, melted

Chopped parsley (optional)

YOU WILL ALSO NEED: WAX PAPER OR ALUMINUM FOIL, LARGE RESEALABLE BAG, COLANDER, 9 X 13-INCH SHALLOW BAKING PAN

1. Preheat the oven to 350°F.
2. Sprinkle cheese on wax paper or foil and dry for 1 hour. Transfer to a large resealable bag. Add flour, salt, and pepper; seal bag and shake to mix.
3. Rinse the potatoes and drain in a colander. Add potatoes to the flour mixture; tightly seal the bag and shake to coat well.
4. Pour butter into the baking pan. Lift potatoes from the bag and arrange them in a single layer in the pan. Sprinkle with parsley, if desired. Roast in the middle or lower third of the oven, turning twice, until browned and crisp and potatoes tender (about 1 hour and 15 minutes).

Carrot Soufflé

MAKES 8 TO 10 SERVINGS

3½ pounds carrots

3 cups sugar

1 tablespoon baking powder

¼ cup all-purpose flour

1 tablespoon vanilla

6 eggs, separated

½ cup (1 stick) butter or margarine, softened

⅛ to ¼ cup powdered sugar

YOU WILL ALSO NEED: BLENDER OR FOOD PROCESSOR, ELECTRIC MIXER, 9 X 12-INCH METAL BAKING DISH (THE SOUFFLÉ WILL NOT RISE WELL IN A GLASS DISH.)

1. Preheat the oven to 350°F.
2. Scrape the carrots and boil until soft, almost falling apart. Drain and purée the carrots.
3. With an electric mixer, beat into carrots the sugar, baking powder, flour, and vanilla. Add egg yolks one at a time, beating thoroughly after each addition. Beat in butter.
4. In separate bowl, beat the egg whites into stiff peaks. Fold into carrot mixture.
5. Bake for 1 hour in metal baking dish. (Fill the baking dish half-full.)
6. Sprinkle top with powdered sugar.

New Orleans Pecan-Praline Cake

PICTURED ON PAGE 96

2½ cups cake flour
1½ teaspoons baking powder
½ teaspoon salt
1 cup (2 sticks) unsalted butter, softened
2 cups sugar
4 large eggs
2 teaspoons vanilla
1 cup whole milk
1½ cups chopped pecans

Syrup

3 tablespoons water
3 tablespoons sugar

Vanilla Cream-Cheese Frosting

12 ounces cream cheese, softened
½ cup (1 stick) unsalted butter, softened
2 teaspoons vanilla
4 cups powdered sugar

Pecan-Praline Topping

1 large egg white
1 tablespoon water
1 cup brown sugar, packed
1½ cups pecan halves

YOU WILL ALSO NEED: 2 9-INCH ROUND CAKE PANS, GREASED; WAX PAPER; WIRE WHISK; MEDIUM BOWL; ELECTRIC MIXER; LARGE BOWL; WIRE RACKS; CAKE PLATTER; RIMMED BAKING SHEET; SMALL SAUCEPAN

1. Position rack in the center of the oven and preheat to 350°F. Line pan bottoms with wax paper, then grease the wax paper.
2. Whisk together flour, baking powder, and salt in a medium bowl.
3. Using an electric mixer, beat butter and sugar in a large bowl until fluffy. Add eggs one at a time, beating until well blended after each addition. Mix in vanilla.
4. Incorporate dry ingredients in 3 additions alternately, with milk in 2 additions, beginning and ending with dry ingredients. Stir in chopped pecans.
5. Divide the batter between the pans. Bake until tester inserted into the center comes out clean and the cakes begin to pull away from sides of the pans (about 35 minutes).
6. Cool the cakes in pans on racks for 10 minutes. If necessary, run a small knife around the pan sides

to loosen the cakes. Turn the cakes onto racks and peel off the wax paper. Brush some of the syrup over the top of the cake. Cool the cakes completely.

7. Transfer 1 cake layer, flat side up, to a platter (using 9-inch diameter tart pan bottoms as a help, if desired). Spread 1 cup of vanilla cream-cheese frosting over the cake layer.

8. Top with a second cake layer, flat side up. Brush the top and sides of the cake with remaining syrup. Spread remaining frosting over top and sides of cake.

9. Sprinkle pecan-praline topping all over the top of the cake, mounding slightly in center, and serve.

Syrup

1. Stir water and sugar in a small saucepan over medium heat until the sugar dissolves and mixture comes to a simmer.

2. Remove from heat and allow to cool.

Vanilla Cream-Cheese Frosting

1. Using electric mixer, beat together cream cheese, butter, and vanilla in a large bowl until smooth.

2. Add powdered sugar 1 cup at a time, beating until smooth after each addition.

Pecan-Praline Topping

1. Preheat the oven to 300°F. Butter a rimmed baking sheet.

2. Using a fork, beat egg white and water in medium bowl until foamy. Add brown sugar and stir until it dissolves. Add pecan halves and toss to coat.

3. Spread pecan mixture on rimmed baking sheet. (Some sugar mixture will flow out onto baking sheet.) Bake until nuts are deep brown and crisp, stirring occasionally, about 10 to 15 minutes.

4. Remove from the oven; stir to loosen nuts from the baking sheet. Cool completely on the baking sheet. (This can be prepared up to 3 days ahead of time and stored in an airtight container at room temperature.)

CANDY'S NOTE: This entire cake can be made a day ahead of time. Store in covered cake dome in the refrigerator. For best results, let stand at room temperature for 1 hour before serving.

My Mother's Fruitcake
MAKES 2 LOAVES; PICTURED ON PAGE 96

2 8-ounce boxes chopped dates
1 16-ounce box candied red cherries, chopped
1 16-ounce box candied green cherries, chopped
1 16-ounce box candied pineapple, chopped

1 pound pecans, chopped
⅔ cup self-rising flour
2 7-ounce cans grated coconut
2 10-ounce cans sweetened, condensed milk

YOU WILL ALSO NEED: 2 TUBE PANS, GREASED AND FLOURED (YOU CAN USE A BUNDT PAN, BUT GREASE AND FLOUR ADEQUATELY, SO CAKE DOESN'T STICK TO PAN.); WAX PAPER OR PARCHMENT; TOOTHPICK

1. Preheat the oven to 325°F. Line the bottoms of tube pans with wax paper or parchment.
2. Combine all ingredients except sweetened, condensed milk, tossing to blend. Add sweetened, condensed milk and mix thoroughly with wooden spoon or with hands.
3. Bake for 1 hour and 15 minutes or until golden brown and toothpick inserted in the center comes out clean.
4. Allow the cakes to cool slightly before removing them from the pans. Store them in an airtight container. The fruitcakes can be stored in the freezer for up to 3 months.

- Plan your Christmas lunch for later in the day, around 2 o'clock, so your morning can be relaxed and enjoyed longer.

- After lunch, take the whole family to see a movie. It's a relaxing way to end a hectic day.

- Try inviting someone new to your Christmas lunch. Look for people at church or work who may not have family nearby with whom to spend the holiday.

- Before bedtime, spend some time reflecting on the blessings of Christmas and the traditions that make it special for your family.

- Fill a jar with jellybeans. Have your guests guess the number of beans in the jar. Winners receive a handmade treat from you!

- Visit a nursing home with a special delivery of candy canes, each with an attached message from your family to the residents and staff.

- If you have the benefit of snowy weather, make snow ice cream!

- Live in a warm climate? No problem, Santa doesn't care. Put out those snowmen decorations and spray your tree with snow. You'll feel the Christmas spirit immediately!

FESTIVE FEAST FOR FEATHERED FRIENDS

YOU WILL NEED:
Non-toxic glue
Wooden frame (new or recycled)
Bag of birdseed
Ribbon
Hot glue gun

1. Spread non-toxic glue on frame. Sprinkle with birdseed, covering the frame thoroughly.

2. Attach a holiday ribbon with hot glue and hang on a tree or an old barn door to dress up the outdoors.

CANDY'S NOTE: This craft will help your feathered friends celebrate the holiday in grand style, and your children will enjoy watching them feast!

CHAPTER Seven

THE
NEW YEAR

The evidences of Christmas have been swept neatly away, and our thoughts are turned to new beginnings. A new year is about to unfold. Sparklers and fireworks on New Year's Eve illuminate a dark sky in celebration, not for what was, but for what will be. Reflections on the past are for the purpose of inspiring the future as families gather on New Year's Day to share resolutions and plans for the next 364 days. Traditional meals (in my family, ham, cabbage, cornbread, and black-eyed peas) are served. It's a quieter time than Christmas…time to play board games and watch parades and football, or just to nap in an easy chair. Though quieter, this is no less a celebration. It's a new year, and the future is waiting!

HAM FOR THE HOLIDAYS

Have you ever inhaled a familiar fragrance that tantalizes all your senses and suddenly find yourself taken back to another time? That is invariably my experience when I smell a ham baking in the oven.

No one could prepare a ham quite like my mother did to celebrate the New Year. The meat cooked for hours, its aroma filling the house until you could almost taste it. I remember one such ham that my mother prepared prior to a New Year's Eve trip our family was taking to my maternal grandmother's house in Dallas, Texas, some six hours away. Although she knew Grandma was preparing a New Year's feast, my mother never likes to go anywhere empty-handed. Her plan was to fully cook the ham, wrap it

well, and secure it in the trunk of our car with the luggage.

My mother had taken great pains to score the ham prettily and colorfully adorn it in golden pineapple rings with crimson cherries in the center of each. It was spectacular! We packed our gifts and belongings into the car and drove off with the thrill of the journey happily guiding our chatter. But before long, the conversation waned drastically as the aroma of that succulent ham filled the car and dominated our thoughts.

Dad steered the car onto the shoulder of the road and flung open the trunk. With Mom's permission, he carved a tiny piece of the ham from an obscure section with his pocketknife. He closed the trunk and returned to evenly divide the tiny morsel between us all; then we drove on.

Of course this didn't satisfy our cravings, and soon we succumbed again…and again…until all that was left of mother's fabulous ham was the bone!

As an adult, New Year's Eve means more to

me than just the traditional ham and family gatherings. It's a time of reflection. And the story of my mother's ham has more than just a humorous purpose.

I ask you, was my mother's ham wasted because it wasn't gloriously displayed on my grandmother's table? I should say not—as intended, it brought great pleasure to her family. But sometimes we lose sight of this principle. If our talents and abilities are not applauded, we feel as though we're failures. But as the woman who broke the alabaster box and poured its priceless contents on Jesus' feet counted His worth greater than that of the box of ointment, so we must be content to pour ourselves out for Him. Even if we're hidden in obscurity, if the things that make us valuable bring pleasure to our Creator, then we have fulfilled our ultimate purpose.

As I approach a new year, the hustle and bustle of Christmas is over. I've met all of my deadlines: cards mailed; gifts purchased, wrapped, received, and returned; menus prepared; and guests entertained. By the time the year ends, my body is aching from all the demands I've placed on it to make the holiday full, and I'm now ready for quiet meditation, looking inward and upward.

The beginning of a new year is the perfect time to assess my strengths as well as my weaknesses and make changes where I can. It's a fresh start, a clean slate, a chapter of my life yet to be written. Empty pages await—new days that I can fill with love, laughter, loyalty, and kindness—days not yet tainted with disappointment, failure, or pain. With each new year, I resolve to yield my will more completely to the loving hand of the Father. I know that as He molds me, I will be conformed in greater measure to His likeness—not to be lauded by the masses, but to bring greater glory to Him.

"He that glorieth, let him glory in the Lord. For not he that commendeth himself is approved, but whom the Lord commendeth."

2 Corinthians 10:17–18

MY NEW YEAR'S REVOLUTION

I was performing a New Year's Eve concert near New Orleans, Louisiana, in the 1980s. As we approached the midnight hour, the pastor addressed the audience. While he spoke, ushers distributed stamped envelopes with blank sheets of paper to the congregation and guests. The minister exhorted us about the power of faith and believing that God is bound by His Word. He encouraged us to believe that miracles would take place in the upcoming year. Then he read aloud from Mark 11:24, "What things soever ye desire, when ye pray, believe that ye receive them, and ye shall have them," and Matthew 18:19, "If two of you shall agree on earth as touching any thing that they shall ask, it shall be done for them of my Father which is in heaven." The pastor asked us to write on our paper everything we wanted God to do for us in the coming year, no matter how great or small the request seemed.

I really couldn't see the importance of writing these things—I figured God had a good memory and knew I had asked for these things many times. But being the invited guest, I felt obligated to take part. While I was going to the trouble to make out a list, I decided to include the really impossible things I had prayed about for years. I listed my secret desires for the deep work of God in the hidden places of my heart, as well as the highest life hurdles I had tried so long to overcome. I threw in a few financial blessings for good measure, then neatly folded my list, sealed it in my self-addressed envelope, and dropped it into the basket passed to me.

The pastor then asked everyone to join hands and lift our hearts in prayer. We began asking God to meet each of our needs, as well as the needs of one another. I felt a sweet presence of the Holy Spirit descend on us. What a glorious way to end a year and enter a new one!

The concert was a success, and several people came forward to make decisions for Christ. We all celebrated the New Year with thunderous joy, eating, laughing, and fellowship until the early morning hours. Then I packed up and journeyed home, forgetting all about those prayer requests. But God didn't forget.

About two years later, I received a letter in the mail. An attached note read, "Please accept our apologies. We are sending your letter back to you a year late. Our congregation moved to a new location, and the box with prayer requests was lost until recently." Immediately I remembered that New Year's Eve in New Orleans, and I nervously unfolded the document I had penned two years earlier. I checked my list of impossible hurdles, deep desires, and the blessings thrown in for good measure. To my utter amazement, I saw that every request had been granted—every miracle had been performed! God had answered each and every prayer.

Philippians 4:19 says, "My God shall supply all your need according to his riches in glory by Christ Jesus." He had supplied all of my needs and even some of my wants!

I don't much believe in New Year's resolutions. But I do believe in the power of God's

Word. I've had a New Year's *revolution*: Instead of making a list of things I plan to change about myself, I prayerfully make a list of things I'd like God to change in me—the impossible and the deep. Then I ask the Lord to do what He promises in His Word and to work His will in my life so I can be pleasing to Him. And if He wants to throw in a few extra blessings for good measure, I'd be happy to receive those too.

"Ask, and it shall be given you; seek, and ye shall find; knock, and it shall be opened unto you: For every one that asketh receiveth; and he that seeketh findeth; and to him that knocketh it shall be opened."

Matthew 7:7–8

My New Year's Prayer

Heavenly Father,
As I cross the threshold of this
Approaching year, fill me with a
Freshness of Your Spirit and an
Acute awareness of Your loving
Kindness to me.
Renew my heart with a song of
Gladness and rejoicing.
Bless my mind with peaceful thanksgiving.
Sweeten my lips with uplifting conversation.
Beautify my person with the joy of salvation.
Grant me wisdom, that it may
Be everlasting life for my soul,
Grace unto my head, and chains of
Restraint about my neck.
Now, dear Lord, give me the strength
To endure the indignities of life
With dignity; for You are my
Confidence, and the knowledge
Of You is my hope.
Amen.

THIS WAS WRITTEN BY MY MOTHER, LaBreeska Hemphill, IN 1986.

Chicken Artichoke Cheese Spread

PICTURED ON PAGE 112

3 cups cooked chicken, diced

2 8-ounce packages cream cheese, softened

1 cup feta cheese, crumbled

1 14-ounce can artichoke hearts, drained and diced

1 cup pecans, finely chopped and toasted

4 green onions, minced

1 tablespoon lemon juice

½ teaspoon salt

1 teaspoon lemon pepper

1 tablespoon garlic, minced

¼ teaspoon basil

Optional Garnish (to create "gift box")

7 to 8 green onion stems

1 red chili pepper, halved

YOU WILL ALSO NEED: Large bowl, 9 x 5-inch loaf pan with straight sides, Plastic wrap, Paper towels, Toothpicks

1. Line the loaf pan with plastic wrap.
2. In a large bowl, stir together all ingredients until blended; spoon into the loaf pan.
3. Cover and chill for 8 hours, or freeze for up to 1 month. Thaw in the refrigerator.
4. Invert the chilled spread onto a serving plate and remove the plastic wrap.
5. Serve with crackers or toasted French baguette slices.

Optional Garnish (to create "gift box")

1. To make this cheese spread into a holiday "gift box," cut the loaf in half crosswise. Place one half directly on top of the other half and smooth the sides, blending together to hide the seam and form the "box."
2. To create the ribbon for your gift box, plunge green onion stems in boiling water, then into ice water to stop the cooking process. Immediately transfer onto paper towels; drain the stems and press between the paper towels to dry.
3. Press onion stems into the sides of the cheese square, beginning with the end of one stem on each side. Bring the stems up and over to the top and center; form loops with the remaining stems and secure in cheese block with wooden picks. Arrange chili pepper halves on top to add more colorful decoration.

Peppercorn-Crusted Beef Tenderloin in Blackjack Sauce

MAKES 4 TO 6 SERVINGS

Beef

¼ cup peppercorn, lightly crushed
1 tablespoon cornstarch
2 teaspoons fresh thyme, chopped
1 teaspoon fresh oregano, chopped
2 tablespoons vegetable oil, divided
1 beef tenderloin (about 2 pounds)
Coarse salt

Blackjack Sauce

1½ pounds beef neck bones

4 large shallots, coarsely chopped
6 cloves garlic, coarsely chopped
2 large carrots, coarsely chopped
1 cup bourbon
1 tablespoon tomato paste
4 sprigs fresh thyme
2 teaspoons peppercorn
2 cups chicken broth
2 cups beef stock or broth
Salt

YOU WILL ALSO NEED: HEAVY SAUCEPAN; FINE SIEVE; SMALL SAUCEPAN; LARGE PLATE; LARGE, OVENPROOF SKILLET; MEAT THERMOMETER

Beef

1. Preheat the oven to 350°F.
2. On a large plate, mix together peppercorn, cornstarch, thyme, and oregano. Brush 1 tablespoon oil over the beef. Roll beef in the peppercorn mixture, coating completely. Season with course salt.
3. Heat remaining 1 tablespoon oil in a large, heavy, ovenproof skillet over medium-high heat. Add the beef and brown on all sides (about 5 minutes). Transfer the skillet to the oven and roast until a meat thermometer inserted into the center of the beef registers 135°F for rare (about 30 minutes) or to desired doneness.
4. Slice the beef and arrange on plates.

Blackjack Sauce

1. Brown beef bones, shallots, garlic, and carrots in a heavy saucepan over medium heat, stirring occasionally, for about 20 minutes. Add the bourbon. Increase heat and boil until the liquid is reduced to one-half (about 5 minutes).
2. Mix in tomato paste, thyme, and peppercorn. Add chicken broth and beef broth or stock. Boil until the liquid is reduced to 1 cup (about 20 minutes).
3. Strain mixture through a fine sieve into a small saucepan. Season with salt.
4. Bring the blackjack sauce to a simmer. Spoon sauce over the beef and serve.

New Year's Luck Peas and Ham
MAKES 6 TO 8 SERVINGS; PICTURED ON PAGE 112

1 pound dried black-eyed peas
½ pound smoked ham, cubed
1 large onion, chopped

Red pepper to taste
3 cloves garlic, minced
Salt to taste

1. Wash the peas and cover them with water; soak overnight.
2. Cook the ham in water until tender. Add peas, onions, red pepper, and garlic; cook slowly (about two hours).
3. Season peas with salt to taste, and serve.

Candy's Best Carrot Cake

PICTURED ON PAGE 112

2 cups all-purpose flour
2 teaspoons baking soda
½ teaspoon salt
2 teaspoons ground cinnamon
3 large eggs
2 cups sugar
¾ cup vegetable oil
¾ cup buttermilk
2 teaspoons vanilla
2 cups grated carrots

1 cup pecans, chopped
1 3½-ounce can of flaked
  coconut
¼ cup pecan halves (optional)
Buttermilk Glaze
1 cup sugar
1½ teaspoons baking soda
½ cup buttermilk
½ cup (1 stick) butter or
  margarine

1 tablespoon light corn syrup
1 teaspoon vanilla
Cream-Cheese Frosting
½ cup (1 stick) butter or
  margarine, softened
11 ounces (1 8-ounce carton
  and 1 3-ounce carton)
  cream cheese, softened
3 cups powdered sugar, sifted
1½ teaspoons vanilla

YOU WILL ALSO NEED: 3 9-INCH ROUND CAKE PANS, WAX PAPER, ELECTRIC MIXER, WOODEN TOOTHPICK, LARGE SAUCEPAN, WIRE RACKS

1. Preheat the oven to 350°F. Line pans with wax paper; lightly grease and flour wax paper. Set aside.
2. Stir together flour, soda, salt, and cinnamon.
3. At medium speed, beat eggs, sugar, and vegetable oil until smooth. Add flour mixture, buttermilk, and vanilla; beating at low speed until blended. Fold in carrots, chopped pecans, and coconut.
4. Pour batter into prepared pans. Bake for 25 to 30 minutes or until a wooden pick inserted in the center comes out clean.
5. Drizzle buttermilk glaze evenly over the cake layers; cool in pans on wire racks for 15 minutes.
6. Remove cake layers from pans and cool completely on wire racks.
7. Spread cream-cheese frosting between layers, then on top and sides of cake. Garnish with pecan halves if desired.

Buttermilk Glaze

1. In large saucepan over medium-high heat, combine all ingredients except vanilla. Boil, stirring often, for 4 minutes.

2. Remove from heat and stir in vanilla.
3. Pour evenly over warm cake layers.

Cream-Cheese Frosting

1. With electric mixer at medium speed, beat together butter and cream cheese until creamy. Add powdered sugar and vanilla; beat until smooth.
2. Frost cake layers as directed.

CANDY'S NOTE: 1 can of crushed pineapple can be added to the cake. My husband, Kent, prefers it without.

Frozen Strawberry Salad
MAKES 8 SERVINGS

1 8-ounce package cream cheese
¾ cup sugar
1 20-ounce can crushed pineapple, drained

2 10-ounce packages frozen strawberries, thawed
1 12-ounce container whipped topping
1 cup chopped pecans or walnuts

YOU WILL ALSO NEED: 9 x 12-INCH BAKING DISH, LIGHTLY GREASED; ELECTRIC MIXER

1. Beat together cream cheese and sugar; stir in pineapple and strawberries. Fold in whipped topping and nuts.
2. Pour mixture into the baking dish. Cover and freeze until firm (about 3 hours).
3. Remove salad from the freezer 30 minutes before serving. Cut into squares.

Holiday Ham
PICTURED ON PAGE 112

1 smoked picnic ham	⅓ cup pineapple juice
1 cup brown sugar	⅓ cup crème de almond

YOU WILL ALSO NEED: LARGE POT, COVERED BAKING DISH

1. Preheat the oven to 400°F.
2. Place the ham in a large pot and cover with water. Bring to a boil, then reduce heat just to the boiling point. Let the ham cook until it's tender but not falling apart. (This removes the salt from the ham.) Remove the ham from the water, let it cool, and slice. Layer ham slices in a covered baking dish.
3. Combine brown sugar, pineapple juice, and crème de almond, mixing thoroughly. Pour the mixture over the ham and cover. Bake for 25 to 30 minutes.

CANDY'S NOTE: This recipe was given to me by my dear friend, Betty Hodges, whom I love very much. She was a wonderful influence in my childhood.

LAGNIAPPE

- Don't forget to kiss your loved ones at midnight! This says, "Congratulations! We've made it through another year."

- Snuggle on the couch with your kids and watch parades on television. It's also fun to work at putting together a big puzzle on a card or coffee table. You can watch the parade and work together.

- When you start putting away the Christmas decorations, leave out anything that is wintry and festive. Snowmen and shiny bows will make those cold January days more fun!

- If a fancy New Year's meal is optional in your family, roast wieners and marshmallows in the fireplace. You could have chili or soup prepared in advance.

- Skip the New Year's resolutions, but don't skip sharing the blessings of the year with family members. Have each person share at least three ways God has blessed them in the past year.

- Invite friends over, but let them know it's a casual party. Have a chili cookoff. The reward is the verbal praise for the best chili.

- Instead of fireworks at midnight, release helium balloons—maybe one for every year of your marriage.

- Sit down and write a brief description of your family. Tuck it away and add to it each year. One day it will mean more to your family than Christmas gifts.

- It's a new year! Start it off right by presenting your family with personalized calendars. This can be done through Office Depot or on your own home computer. Make it more special by including the birthdays and anniversaries of all family members as well as any activities already scheduled for the year. Pictures of loved ones can be used to depict each changing month and season. The fun project will delight family members all year.

- As a family write down your goals for the year. Include things that you want to do as a family and things that you want God to bless you with or help you change.

- Record a New Year's blessing on your answering machine.

Thanks for Auld Lang Syne

To all the friends I've loved in life, to those far from me:
The road we traveled veered somewhere, a turn we couldn't see.
It must have been so gradual, maybe one step at a time.
I'm sorry I was too busy with life to notice you weren't in mine.
You that I've known so keenly, shared secrets and so much fun,
It's like I've lost you in a forest and don't know which way to run.
To all the friends I've loved in life, I'll say without regret:
"I loved you then, I love you now; my heart cannot forget."
The good in you helped mold the soul that I have come to be;
So I carry a part of you in the heart of me.
Wherever you are in this world, I hope that life is kind.
To all the friends I've loved and lost: "Thanks for auld lang syne."

CANDY CHRISTMAS